To Ann + Geoff

GROSSI FLORENTINO
Secrets & Recipes

RECIPES AND FOOD BY GUY GROSSI

STORY BY JAN McGUINNESS

PHOTOGRAPHY BY ADRIAN LANDER

LANTERN
an imprint of
PENGUIN BOOKS

LANTERN

Published by the Penguin Group
Penguin Group (Australia)
250 Camberwell Road, Camberwell, Victoria 3124, Australia
(a division of Pearson Australia Group Pty Ltd)
Penguin Group (USA) Inc.
375 Hudson Street, New York, New York 10014, USA
Penguin Group (Canada)
90 Eglinton Avenue East, Suite 700, Toronto ON M4P 2Y3, Canada
(a division of Pearson Penguin Canada Inc.)
Penguin Books Ltd
80 Strand, London WC2R 0RL England
Penguin Ireland
25 St Stephen's Green, Dublin 2, Ireland
(a division of Penguin Books Ltd)
Penguin Books India Pvt Ltd
11 Community Centre, Panchsheel Park, New Delhi – 110 017, India
Penguin Group (NZ)
67 Apollo Drive, Mairangi Bay, Auckland 1310, New Zealand
(a division of Pearson New Zealand Ltd)
Penguin Books (South Africa) (Pty) Ltd
24 Sturdee Avenue, Rosebank, Johannesburg 2196, South Africa

Penguin Books Ltd, Registered Offices: 80 Strand, London, WC2R 0RL, England

First published by Penguin Books Australia Ltd, 2003
This paperback edition published by Penguin Group (Australia), 2007

1 3 5 7 9 10 8 6 4 2

Cover design by Cathy Larsen © Penguin Group (Australia)
Internal design by Leonie Stott
Typeset in Fairfield Light and Helvetica Thin by Post Pre-press, Brisbane, Queensland
Printed in Singapore by Imago Productions

National Library of Australia
Cataloguing-in-Publication data:

Grossi, Guy, 1965– .
Grossi Florentino : secrets and recipes.
Includes index.
ISBN-13: 978 1 920989 71 2.
ISBN-10: 1 920989 71 4.
1. Florentino (Restaurant : Melbourne, Vic.) – History.
2. Grossi Florentino (Restaurant : Melbourne, Vic.) – History.
3. Cookery, Italian. 4. Restaurants – Victoria –
Melbourne – History. I. McGuinness, Jan, 1946– .
II. Grossi Florentino (Restaurant : Melbourne, Vic.). III. Title.

641.5945

www.penguin.com.au

Endpapers: Mural at Grossi Florentino photographed by John Romeo

To my father, Pietro.
His discipline and love have given me strength.

GUY GROSSI

Contents

Introduction

Italians live to eat. The enjoyment of food and the care, knowledge, warmth and hospitality surrounding it are at the forefront of their culture and are transported with them wherever they settle around the globe.

Melbourne's rich tradition of Italian cuisine blossomed in the period of post-World War II immigration, but is grounded firmly in the service and hospitality established in the 1920s and '30s in the restaurants of a few close-knit family groups who forever changed Australia's eating habits. Cafe (now Grossi) Florentino – or Flo's, as it is known affectionately – is the only one of these restaurants remaining. Well into its eighth decade, it is Melbourne's and indeed Australia's oldest and best-known restaurant business. Grossi Florentino is not one but three restaurants that cater for every stratum of society. It is a collection of little worlds within a world, each offering its own pleasures and wrapped in its own memories, frequented by an overlapping clientele of devotees.

Grossi Florentino occupies the site of Melbourne's first licensed wine bar, opened in 1900, and its evolution to a world-class restaurant parallels not merely the culinary but the social, cultural and economic twentieth-century life of the city. At this most Italian of Italian establishments Australians first tasted cassata, experienced bistro dining and were introduced to espresso coffee. As early as 1929, Cafe Florentino's founder, Rinaldo Massoni, installed an enormous silver-plated apparatus that huffed and puffed, emitting gusts of steam and delicious coffee aromas in equal measure, until replaced with a more 'modern' machine imported from Milan in 1940. The success of Il Bistro (now the Cellar Bar) in the 1950s provoked changes to Victoria's liquor laws, with the bistro referred to in *Hansard*. Beyond such innovations, the Florentino's fame and influence have spread throughout Melbourne and Australia via the many eating places established by its former staff.

Apart from its well-known employees and chefs, generations of prime ministers, entrepreneurs, industry leaders, local and international celebrities, the old rich and nouveau riche have graced the premises at 78–82 Bourke Street. They were and continue to be drawn by the charm and bustle overlaying the essential combination of good food, wine and conversation – which, in Italian hands, is the antithesis of hushed grandeur, no matter how elegant the surroundings. Indeed, if the walls could talk the words would be a babble about the famous and infamous, encapsulating more than 100 years of history.

What follows is the story of a revered institution that has become woven into the national social fabric. It is a tribute to all those who have contributed to its iconic status, from owners and staff to chefs and patrons, past and present. It is a celebration for those who know and love Grossi Florentino and an enticement for those who would like to – not least through Guy Grossi's recipes, drawn from every corner of the Florentino's operation.

La Storia

A building at 82 Bourke Street – described as a brick house with four rooms and kitchen, occupied by a Dr Philips – first appeared in the Melbourne rate book in 1853.

Seven years later, brick houses were built at numbers 78 and 80 as part of a terrace of eight erected for Moses Benjamin, a prominent merchant in Melbourne's early commercial development. The terrace housed various businesses and residences, including Edments Fancy Goods Store and Benjamin's Drapers Shop, with number 78 converting to Melbourne's first wine saloon at the turn of the century.

The history (*la storia*) of Grossi Florentino really began eighteen years later, when Samuel Wynn took over the Colonial Wine Shop at numbers 78 and 80 from a French couple called Moureau. 'Colonial' meant the shop was licensed to sell only Australian-made wines and no beer or spirits. While it did stock quality table wines, the demand was for fortified sweet reds and whites, such as port and muscat. The most fashionable of these was madeira.

'In those days, wine saloons were not only numerous, they were often less than respectable,' wrote Allan Wynn in *The Fortunes of Samuel Wynn*, his biography of his father. 'Many were furnished with pianos and "gay young ladies" and the customers were known at times to transcend the limits of propriety. The Bourke Street shop was run differently. The front was modernised, the bottle department was partitioned from the bar and, quickly, the customers became more numerous and behaviour more decorous, though it was never stilted.'

Samuel Wynn was a Polish Jew originally called Weintraub, and he and his family lived upstairs in what is now the Wynn Room, where one of his sons, David, learned to tell the time on the still-present wall clock. Sammy ran two bars, one facing Bourke Street and frequented by politicians from the neighbouring Parliament (the seat of the federal government until 1927), the other at the rear and favoured by homeless men from the nearby Gordon House shelter. He claimed to serve two types of derelict and to prefer the latter.

PREVIOUS PAGES The Mural Room in 1934, the year it opened. The unknown photographer has taken two pictures to capture the entire room and then spliced them together – so it appears here much wider than it actually is.

5

ABOVE **Samuel Wynn,**
proprietor of the wine shop
at 78–80 Bourke Street –
the predecessor of
Cafe Florentino.

By 1928, Sammy had prospered sufficiently to concentrate on wine growing and winemaking, eventually moving on to salvage the Coonawarra Estate vineyard from destruction and to create a great wine company. But before all that he established Cafe Denat, the precursor to Cafe Florentino, in his family's former living quarters.

Cafe Denat, a French Edwardian establishment, was much patronised by 'very easy women', according to the late George Tsindos, a subsequent Cafe Florentino owner. Denat was an unlicensed cafe, so Wynn's became its major source of wines. But in 1920, according to Allan's record of events, Monsieur Denat retired. Fearful of losing such a major outlet for his wines, Sammy Wynn accepted Denat's offer to buy the cafe and ran it in partnership with the head waiter, George Hildebrant, until 1924, when exhaustion prompted consolidation in Bourke Street.

George Tsindos's less sanitised version of events is that the police closed Denat down for selling wine without a licence and, under the terms of the prevailing wine licence, the restaurant required a bar, two toilets, at least two bathrooms, two places for tethering horses and a dining room – all of which Sammy Wynn could provide.

Whatever the circumstances, Cafe Denat moved in above the Colonial Wine Shop in 1924 and continued there until 1928 under a succession of managers. George says 'Cafe Denat' was still on the door and picked out on the front tiles until around 1960, when a customer slipped and fell and sued the management – a long time after Rinaldo Massoni had acquired the lease and renamed the restaurant Cafe Florentino. Whether he acquired it with a £500 loan from his aunt Velia Virgona (mother of Mario, founder of Fitzroy's Casa Virgona) or in partnership with four other Italians – including Salvatore, the Florentino's first and most famous chef – depends on the source. George, then a waiter, vouched for the short-lived partnership, which was 'bizarre and argumentative'. Massoni, he said, needed funds to buy the others out and got them from Pierre Funari, a regular patron and dress designer at Georges department store.

A surgical instrument maker by trade, Rinaldo had arrived in Melbourne from Lucca, near Florence, in 1911. He worked for Ramsay & Co. until he damaged an eye after a bit of metal became lodged in it, prompting a move into hospitality that was orchestrated by his in-laws. Rinaldo had married Grace Watson, whose parents Ella (née

Panelli) and James owned a wine shop in Fitzroy and whose brother Jimmy, in the 1930s, started the well-known Carlton wine bar and restaurant that bears his name still (also with financial help from canny Aunt Velia).

In 1924, after a lonely stint running a wine shop in Geelong, where there weren't many Italians, Rinaldo bought the Cafe Latin (formerly Cafe Bella) in Exhibition Street with a friend from Lucca, Camillo Triaca. Camillo remained to establish that subsequently famous business, while Massoni moved in 1927 to a wine shop in Elgin Street, Carlton, before finally taking over at Cafe Denat. There he changed the style to Italian and the name to Cafe Florentino. Originally, Rinaldo opted for 'Cafe Florence', according to his son Leon. But the family thought it should be something more lyrical and suggested the Italian *fiorentino*, meaning 'of Florence'. This, being thought difficult for Australians to pronounce, was anglicised as Florentino.

'Dad got word that the Denat was going broke and approached Sammy Wynn,' says Leon. 'In fact, the cafe had been closed for some months, so he got it rent free for the first six months.' Under Rinaldo's management, the new Cafe Florentino never looked back. Within six years he had expanded it by adding the elegant and sumptuously decorated Mural Room, and by the end of the 1930s the restaurant was enjoying an international reputation.

The number of theatres in Spring and Exhibition Streets, and the proximity of Parliament, had encouraged Italian immigrants to create a restaurant district at the far end of the city. By the 1930s, Cafe Florentino's neighbours and competitors included Cafe Latin in Exhibition Street, Cafe d'Italia in Lonsdale Street and the Society across the road in Bourke Street. With the hotel dining rooms at Scotts, Menzies, the Australia, Melbourne Club Hotel (Mario's) and the Windsor, these restaurants more or less constituted Melbourne's city-based dining-out scene then and for a few decades to come.

In those days dining out was the preserve of a sophisticated minority of intellectuals, actors and artists, journalists, writers, businessmen, politicians and establishment figures. Everyone else was tucked up in the suburbs eating chops and three veg, and there they remained, more or less, until Victoria's liquor laws were liberalised and BYOs were introduced in 1968.

BELOW Rinaldo Massoni enjoys a glass of wine with staff and guests at a party in the Wynn Room, early 1930s.

Florentino

In the mid-1930s a three-course meal with a 135 ml bottle of wine cost the equivalent of 36 cents in the inside (Mural) room and 26 cents in the less formal (Wynn) room, with 5 cents considered a gigantic tip. Rinaldo's philosophy was 'Serve good-quality food at fair prices, break even on the food, and make money on the wine'. Rarely a soul was seen above Swanston Street then, and patrons could angle-park in Bourke Street, where, as at the top of Lonsdale and in Exhibition and Spring Streets, small tradesmen proliferated amid shopfronts filled with empty chocolate boxes. These shopfronts, according to George Tsindos, indicated brothels, and there were about 100 of them in among the small engineering firms, wire works and plumbing businesses. The going rate was higher on Bourke Street but declined, as did the quality of the gin, the closer one got to Lonsdale Street.

While **not the most salubrious end of town**, it was certainly colourful. Indeed, Allan Wynn relates how A.H. Spencer, when he opened the Hill of Content bookshop next to Wynn's in 1922, likened the area to the darker part of Montmartre, where 'gangsters soft-footed the byways, revolver shots sounded their echoes, worshippers of Bacchus sang or moaned their melodies, making midnight and the a.m. eerily mysterious'. The Hill of Content quickly became (and remains) one of Melbourne's finest bookshops. Frequented by Spencer's far-from-shady friends, and patrons including the painters Arthur Streeton and Tom Roberts and most of the Lindsay family, Dame Nellie Melba and Sir John Monash, it lifted the area's tone.

In 1933 George Tsindos, a twenty-year-old drinks waiter who had migrated from Cyprus seven years earlier, joined Cafe Florentino – an involvement, both as employee and owner, that was to span almost fifty years. George, whom Rinaldo always called 'Greco', claims Rinaldo treated him as a son. 'Whenever the family had a party at the restaurant they always wanted me to look after them,' said George. 'I learned a lot from Rinaldo. He trusted me and I did all the messages.' When George's son Raymond was born prematurely and needed special care, Rinaldo supported him, paying all the bills but for a token amount.

World War II interrupted George's career in 1941. A bout of rheumatic fever made him unfit to fight, so he performed essential service in a munitions factory until

9

he was advised to leave the city for his health. George and his wife, Mabel, then took over a guesthouse at Sorrento on the Mornington Peninsula.

Rinaldo died suddenly of a heart attack in 1941 and the business was held in trust until Leon reached his majority in 1946. Young, inexperienced and put upon by staff and customers alike, Leon had soon had enough of coping alone and in September 1950 he approached George, who, as it happened, had had enough of Sorrento and was planning to take over a hotel in Albury. Instead, he and Leon formed a partnership that lasted until 1963 and expanded the business to include the Cellar Bar and Bistro Grill.

Still young enough to do something else, Leon again tired of his inheritance and the partnership was dissolved in what lawyers Blake and Riggall (now Blake Dawson Waldron) described as the most amicable handover they had ever settled: George and Leon simply sat down after lunch one day and bid for the other's share of the business until one accepted the figure reached. Leon accepted first, although George said later that he had been prepared to go higher. After a stint as a wine merchant, Leon went on to own and run many successful restaurants, including Cafe Balzac, Tolarno Bistro and Ristorante Massoni, and to establish an award-winning vineyard on the Mornington Peninsula.

Back in Bourke Street, with George at the helm, the Florentino played host to a daily stream of celebrities, politicians and the cream of Melbourne society. The business continued to prosper and its reputation firmed as **the country's best Italian restaurant**, famous for its crêpes and chocolate soufflé. It is said that tears flowed when the staff were told of the restaurant's impending sale to Branco Tocigl in 1979, thus ending a long association with the Tsindos family. But Branco, born in Trieste and schooled in Melbourne's dining habits, first as a drinks waiter at Mario's and later as food and beverage manager of the Southern Cross Hotel, understood the Florentino's winning formula and did little to change it.

Only failing health and an offer too good to refuse enticed Branco to sell to property developer Floyd Podgornik in the late 1980s. Renovations were long overdue and Floyd proceeded to update and restore every section of the business with an (eventually) sympathetic touch. He was a high-flying entrepreneur with a complicated business

OPPOSITE Il Bistro, looking atypically deserted, in a photograph styled by Leon Massoni in the 1950s, complete with an advertisement for Wynvale Flagons on the window and Massoni's name etched above the door.
Photo: Gerd Rosskamp

and personal life. Within months of reopening the refurbished Cafe Florentino, he committed suicide. His widow, Lorraine, took over the Florentino in the early 1990s after a much-publicised tussle for control with Floyd's girlfriend, Carolyn Palliardi.

Lorraine kept the place alive during a difficult decade that saw the closure of most of Melbourne's grand restaurants. In March 1999 she handed over the reigns to the Grossi family, one of the few Italian families still involved in running restaurants.

Pietro Grossi had arrived in Melbourne in May 1960, enticed from Milan by Mario Vigano to work as a chef at Mario's. On his first day there, six of the staff took him around the corner to the Florentino for lunch. They included Branco Tocigl, who advised Pietro that to be a good Aussie he must drink beer and play the horses. While this didn't make much of an impression, the Florentino – which opened, by coincidence, in the year of his birth – affected him as it has so many others down the years. He resolved then and there to own it one day. This gave him a goal, he said, which was eventually reached through hard work and the ownership of several family restaurants, including Caffe Grossi, Pietro's and Epoca. Along the way, he cooked for Leon Massoni at Tolarno Bistro and was a partner in Ristorante Massoni, where his son, Guy, did his apprenticeship.

Pietro retired just before the family took over the Florentino, but still basked in the achievement. As Guy says, 'This didn't happen by accident – it was planned from day one.' The Grossis have invigorated and restored authenticity to every aspect of the Florentino's menu, wine list and ambience, and thus the circle has closed. The Florentino is back in the hands of an Italian family and the Grossis have achieved their long-held ambition to own it.

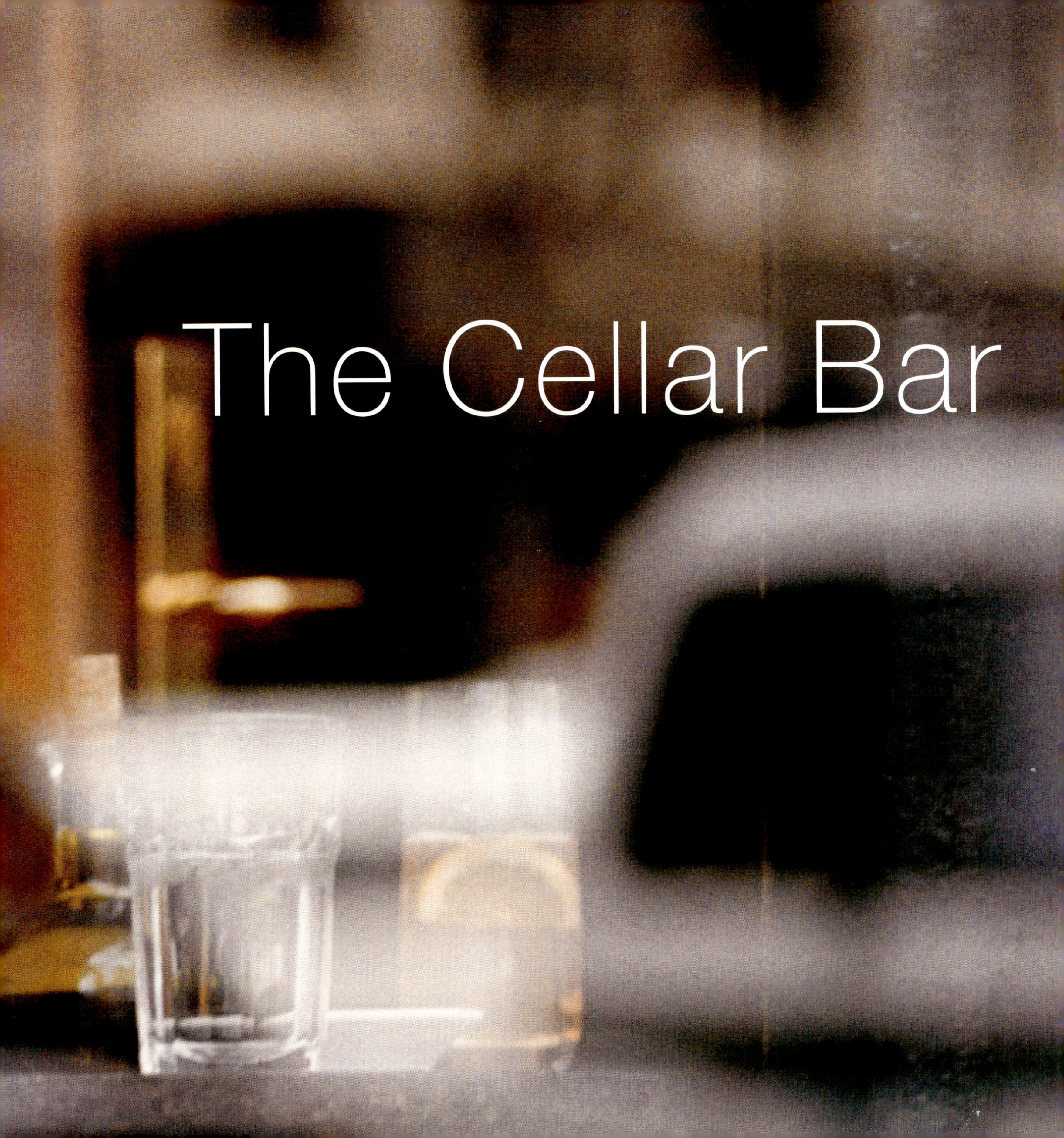
The Cellar Bar

The Cellar Bar is the shopfront of Grossi Florentino, a high-traffic area where the mood is always changing. Whether bustling and businesslike in the morning, assertive and noisy around lunchtime or sexy and romantic in the evening, it's the stage upon which Melbourne cafe society struts its stuff.

From the day it opened in the mid-1950s, the Cellar Bar has been a magnet for the habitués of high and low bohemia, businesspeople, professionals and politicians, taxi drivers, journalists, actors and artists. 'This is our place – you get the coffee you want, the boss comes in and everyone knows you by name,' says Stefan Aralica, who has been there every day since 1971, when curiosity about the crowd around the bar drew him in the door.

Advertising industry doyen and horse breeder Charles Anzarat stops in around 9.30 a.m. on his way from Toorak to his city office as he has done for twenty years, resplendent in a three-piece suit and sporting a fresh buttonhole. Between 10 and 11 a.m. a group of cabbies gathers for morning coffee; twenty-five years ago the attraction was Lydia, the buxom barista, now it's the company and familiarity. They say you nod to anyone you don't know and after about five years you'll probably speak to them.

Politicians past and present are among the blow-ins. Bob Hawke drops by to pick up a newspaper and study the racing form, or to salute long-time barista Elda D'Amico with a 'You make beautiful coffee, signora', while Paul Keating stops for a coffee before or after his visits to the Hill of Content bookshop. Former parliamentarians Gareth Evans, John Button and Barry Jones are frequent visitors, as are politicians from the neighbouring State Parliament, AFL footballers, actors including Geoffrey Rush, and staffers from Liberal Party headquarters around the corner.

It is a tableau of relaxed good fellowship, a scene, a ritual, a tradition repeated in elegant bars on every Italian main square and along the streets and alleyways of every Italian town and city. The Florentino's Cellar Bar has been much imitated, particularly in Melbourne, but never equalled. Here an **authentic cafe society** is alive and well and strongly linked to the city's past.

The Cellar Bar opened as 'Il Bistro' on the site of Melbourne's first wine bar and Sammy Wynn's old wine shop. The homeless men from nearby Gordon House had frequented the old wine bar for years, hooked on cheap plonk, warmed by an old kerosene heater and fed on heated leftovers from the upstairs kitchen. But it barely paid its way and something had to be done, recalls Leon Massoni. George Tsindos subscribed to *Realities*, a glossy French lifestyle magazine where the talk was of the new bistros in Paris and Lyon. *Bistro* is Russian for 'fast', Leon discovered, after seeing the word on a cafe in Prahran, and he Italianised it with *Il* (meaning 'the'). David Wynn, who still owned the building, cooperated in the conversion, donating a food-serving hatch made by sculptor Clifford Last in the shape of a giant wine barrel festooned with grapes.

Leon insists Il Bistro opened in 1954, while George cited 19 May 1956 – in time for the Olympic Games – as the precise date, and a document shows the business name was registered on 29 May 1956. Neither Leon nor George disputes that it was an instant success and a goldmine upon which the rest of the enterprise came to depend in tough times. Originally, Il Bistro opened only for lunch and closed at 3 p.m. – although this didn't prevent the advertising fraternity drinking on until 5 p.m. It served **fast food and cheap wine** and was so popular that people queued outside. A narrow wall shelf (still there) was for resting your drink when it was standing room only. The crush within was often so thick that patrons even stood in the street eating their pasta and drinking wine in defiance of the prevailing by-laws. Caught up in the conversion, George forgot to notify the Licensing Court of the wine bar's change of business. However, the judge was well known to the Florentino and when an inspector came to review the *fait accompli* he advised merely that a sharp coat-hook needed rounding off.

Il Bistro was so popular that it changed Victoria's drinking laws and was cited in *Hansard*. Until the mid-1950s wine bars were licensed under the Australian Wine

Licence to sell only Australian wines, but with Il Bistro's success the Liquor Control Commission decreed that wine bars must choose between becoming restaurants or bottle shops (selling only Australian wines). Needless to say, that was the end of wine bars. Leon led the way and his wine-bar-owning relatives Jimmy Watson and Mario Virgona quickly followed suit into the (official) wine and food business.

At Il Bistro the food was simple and limited – pasta and a meat or chicken special, plus buttered rolls and a selection of cold fillings – and wine-based products were the only liquor served. Since liquor could only be consumed with meals, diehard customers would nominate one of their number to buy food and the rest would drink. Right up until the Grossis introduced table service, patrons ordered and received a docket at the bar, which they then presented at the serving hatch. At a time when pubs were drinking houses awash with beer, there was nothing else remotely like Il Bistro. And so this small slice of European sophistication became a magnet for a very young crowd of students, artists from the top end of town where rents were still cheap, journalists from across the road at radio 3UZ and the nearby Herald & Weekly Times building, stockbrokers and solicitors. 'For many it was a learning curve. They cut their teeth on Il Bistro and then moved on,' says Raymond Tsindos. 'Their progress through the Florentino's four rooms is a study of people growing up.'

Bar stools along the timber-panelled walls were modelled on those in the Italian ocean liners then visiting Melbourne. Originally the bar was at the front, where a desiccated ('stuffed' is too flattering a description) alligator occupied pride of place in the window and was later joined by various rubber plants, with chairs and tables down the back. This arrangement was reversed and more space opened up during the Podgornik renovation, but in the old days it made Il Bistro an extremely cosy and highly desirable lunch spot. It was a case of 'come early and get a seat', with those arriving after midday having no hope.

Back then, Saturday lunch was almost a non-event. However, Il Bistro soon became the place to meet late on Saturday mornings for a glass of wine and something hot before strolling to the Melbourne Cricket Ground or whiling away the afternoon chatting and perusing the weekend papers. 'When the tables were still at the back,

ABOVE The chic reputation of the Florentino meant that it was in demand for fashion shoots, as in this photograph from the 1960s.

Photo: Kurt Veld and Jon Van Gaalen

everyone knew whose each table was, which chair they were going to sit on and what they would eat,' recalls Stefan. 'It was standing room only and once you got in, you couldn't get out.'

Lunches, Saturday or otherwise, were always popular. Until the Grossis expanded the menu, they centred on a daily pasta special advertised on a blackboard in the window. Monday was rigatoni, Tuesday cannelloni, Wednesday tagliatelle, Thursday lasagne and Friday gnocchi, says property consultant Andy Sinn, who has trammed up-town to lunch at the Cellar Bar every weekday for over forty years (but never before 2 p.m., to avoid the crush) – except when forced by Floyd Podgornik's renovations to patronise Pellegrinis, which, he says, didn't suit him at all.

Actor and writer Philip Jones has held court with his mates every Wednesday lunchtime for more than thirty years, including at one time his Labrador, Charlie, who was allowed to sit just inside the door. Philip recalls that a group including arts patron John Reed, art dealer Georges Mora and David Wynn met every Friday in the 1960s for gnocchi. 'Soft on the inside, crisp on the outside, served with butter and Parmesan, it was one of the great dishes,' says Jones. 'It was so good that if there was anyone in town Georges wanted to impress he'd take them to Il Bistro for Romana semolina gnocchi.'

The Il Bistro barrel and name are still there, together with a plaque advising patrons how to order. According to the regulars, the plaque has looked 'a bit wonky' since the early 1980s, when it fell off and struck a female patron who was in the process of fetching a plate of lasagne. Branco Tocigl was the owner then and he placated the customer with a bottle of champagne.

Those for whom drinking was the priority became known as the 'riesling people', the 'moselle people', even the 'sauternes people', depending on their favourite tipple. Sometime in the 1970s, a special Cellar Bar negroni was invented. Elda D'Amico remembers making this very popular variation on the Italian cocktail by the dozen and says it's still requested occasionally. Arriving at the Cellar Bar from the sleepy and stuffy surrounds of the Australian Club in 1979, Elda was overwhelmed by the roar of conversation and bonhomie on her first day behind the bar. Clearly nervous, she took an order for a Campari and while she was mixing it the patron disappeared, only to return with a long-stemmed rose

from the florist opposite, which he presented, saying, 'Welcome.' Elda says that it was such fun working at Il Bistro that no one who got a job there ever left.

What Elda has seen and experienced deserves a book of its own. There was the patient from nearby St Vincent's Hospital, for example, who absented himself from the hospital at lunchtimes to drink at the Cellar Bar, resplendent in pyjama bottoms and a jumper. He met a group near the door on his first escapade, they shouted him, and he became a mate and returned to drink with them every day for about a week.

Others fell under the Cellar Bar's spell with messier results, like the two regulars, one male and one female, who introduced themselves and began meeting two or three times a week despite both being married to other people. Things developed and before long they were at the bar together every morning, while the man, to the embarrassment of all, continued going there every other afternoon with his wife. This went on for a couple of years, with the wife less and less in evidence, until finally that marriage ended. A few months later the woman left her husband, but by then the man had met someone new, who he subsequently married! None of the parties has been seen since.

Today the food of the Cellar Bar is simple and professionally executed but in the *casalinga* (home-cooked) style. The menu is eclectic – from snacks to substantial mains and cakes and pastries – and is designed to fit the mood and needs of the clientele, from breakfast to supper. Sammy Wynn would be astounded not only by the food, but by the sophistication and range of beverages served in his simple wine shop. Despite the changes, the renovations and the passing years, something of the old bohemian bonhomie lingers on in this narrow space where dispensing hospitality has been the only business for more than a century.

At nights, the Cellar Bar plays host to a different cast of characters. The buzz of activity is often enlivened by a few late stayers as the after-theatre crowd gathers for supper and businessmen leaving the restaurant upstairs or passing by on the street are drawn in for a last coffee and cognac. It is here that Guy Grossi comes to relax and linger after a hard night's work in the kitchen. When the doors finally close at around midnight, it's likely to be on the boss – who, like so many others around town, regards the Cellar Bar as his special place.

Sarde gratinate con fichi – Local sardines filled with breadcrumbs and herbs, wrapped in speck, with roasted figs

When they are fresh and at their best, sardines are a fantastic fish. The flesh should be firm and the eyes glossy and protruding – the fish should look like they are still alive. Local Melbourne sardines are great because they come in a great variety, but they can be difficult to obtain, especially if the weather is poor. In the Veneto a sweet-and-sour onion and saffron dressing called *saor* is fabulous with sardines; in Sicily a similar dish is called *scapece*. My version reflects Sicilian tones, with the freshness of the fish enhanced by the herbs and speck. ∾ *Serves 4 as an entrée or 2–3 as a main meal*

olive oil

1 clove garlic, chopped

500 g fresh breadcrumbs

75 g speck, chopped

3 pinches freshly chopped flat-leaf parsley

6 sage leaves, chopped

6 mint leaves, chopped

sea salt and freshly ground black pepper

freshly grated Parmigiano-Reggiano

12 fresh sardines

12 thin slices speck (extra)

6 figs, peeled

Preheat the oven to 200°C. Put 100 ml olive oil in a frying pan and add the garlic, breadcrumbs and chopped speck. Allow to fry together. Add the herbs, season with salt and pepper and continue to fry until the mixture looks 'sandy'. Remove from the heat and allow to cool. Add Parmigiano-Reggiano to taste and mix well.

Leaving the head and tail intact, gently remove the bones from the centre of each sardine – first, using a boning knife, lift the bones away from the flesh, then run your fingers between the flesh and the main bone, and snap the bone close to the tail and then close to the head. (If you prefer, you can ask your fishmonger to bone the sardines.) Spoon some breadcrumb mixture into each sardine and wrap the fish in a slice of speck. Sprinkle a little more breadcrumb mixture on an oven tray and arrange the sardines on top. Cover the fish with the remaining breadcrumb mixture and drizzle generously with olive oil. Bake for 10–15 minutes or until golden.

Meanwhile, put the figs in a separate oven tray or ovenproof baking dish with a little olive oil. Season lightly with salt and pepper and bake for 5–10 minutes. Serve the sardines with the figs as a garnish.

VARIATION: Add some sultanas and pine nuts to the breadcrumb mixture for an interesting twist.

Panzarotti – Fontina-filled bread, deep-fried

When I was growing up, my mother would cook these as an after-school snack for me and my brother and sisters, and we would eat them as we played. She would add chopped ham and other ingredients to the filling. In Piazza delle Erbe in Verona, my mother's home town, the street vendors still sell piping-hot *panzarotti*. Great in the winter! ❧ *Makes 12*

30 g fresh yeast

200 ml lukewarm water

olive oil

pinch of salt

500 g flour

FONTINA FILLING

100 g butter

100 g flour

300 ml milk

sea salt and freshly ground black pepper

2–3 grates of fresh nutmeg

250 g fontina cheese, freshly grated

In a large bowl, dissolve the yeast in the water. Add 1 tablespoon olive oil and the salt. Stir in the flour and combine to form a dough. Turn out onto your workbench and knead for 10 minutes. Cover, put in a warm place and leave to rise for 1 hour or until the mixture has doubled in size.

To make the filling, melt the butter in a saucepan over moderate heat. Add the flour and cook until the mixture changes colour. Pour in the milk and whisk until well blended. Season with salt, pepper and nutmeg, then reduce the heat and cook for approximately 10 minutes, stirring gently, until the mixture thickens. Add the cheese and stir well. Allow to cool.

Roll out the dough on a floured surface to form a thin sheet (3 mm), folding as necessary as you roll. Cut into rounds approximately 15 cm in diameter. Place some filling in the centre, fold the dough over and brush a little water on the edges to seal. The parcels will be shaped like half-moons.

Deep-fry the parcels in hot olive oil in 2–3 batches for about 3 minutes until golden brown, moving them around as they fry. Drain on paper towel and serve immediately.

Piadina e condimenti – Grilled flatbread with various accompaniments

Piadina is a traditional bread of Emilia-Romagna. The recipe is simple and very quick to make. My problem is I can't stop eating it! I serve it with *baccalà* (see opposite) and other pastes, and it's also great with stracchino cheese and prosciutto. But it's a terrific way to dress up a vast number of goodies for a tasty snack, and you could use almost anything out of the pantry. Use a good-quality extra-virgin olive oil when making pastes such as those that follow, as the flavour of the oil will be obvious and will add great depth. ❧ *Makes about 8*

30 g fresh yeast

500 g flour

pinch of salt

50 g softened lard *or* butter

2 teaspoons olive oil

water

Dissolve the yeast in a little warm water, then put it in a bowl with the flour and salt. Mix in the lard and olive oil and enough water to form a soft dough. Knead for 10 minutes, then cover and allow to rest for 1 hour.

Preheat the char-grill or a ribbed pan over a moderate heat. Break off pieces of dough about the size of your fist and roll them out on a floured surface to rounds about 5 mm thick. Brush the hot grill or pan with a little olive oil and cook the rounds for 1–2 minutes on each side. Spread with your desired paste and eat immediately.

PURE DI ACCIUGHE (ANCHOVY PASTE)

6 slices fresh casalinga bread, crusts removed

olive oil

1 clove garlic, chopped

250 g good-quality anchovies in olive oil (or more for a stronger paste), drained

3 pinches freshly chopped flat-leaf parsley

extra-virgin olive oil

To make the anchovy paste, cut the bread into cubes. Put some olive oil in a frying pan and sauté the garlic until it begins to colour. Add the anchovies and toss until very soft. Add the bread and parsley. Toss and cook for a further 3–5 minutes to allow the flavours to combine. Cool. Put the cooled bread-and-anchovy mixture in a blender and blend, drizzling in a little extra-virgin olive oil, until you have a smooth, homogenised paste. The paste will keep for 1 week in an airtight container in the refrigerator. ❧ *Makes 400 g*

PURE DI FAVE (BROAD-BEAN PASTE)

olive oil

1 clove garlic, chopped

1 onion, chopped

500 g dried broad beans, soaked overnight
and drained

sea salt and freshly ground black pepper

2–3 sage leaves, chopped

2 bay leaves

2 litres water

extra-virgin olive oil

BACCALÀ MANTECATO (SALTED-COD PASTE)

1 side (approximately 400 g) of baccalà

olive oil

½ onion, finely chopped

1 clove garlic, sliced

25 g fresh white bread slices, crusts removed

dash of dry white wine

½ cup freshly chopped flat-leaf parsley

pinch of freshly ground black pepper

250 ml cream

100 ml extra-virgin olive oil

dash of verjuice

To make the broad-bean paste, put a little olive oil in a large pot and add the garlic and onion. Sauté until translucent. Add the beans and toss to distribute the ingredients evenly. Add salt and pepper to taste, and the sage and bay leaves. Pour in the water and simmer gently for about 1 hour until the beans are totally soft. You may need to add more water during the cooking process. Cool. Discard the bay leaves. Purée the cooled beans in a food processor and pass the purée through a sieve. Add extra-virgin olive oil to moisten as required. The paste will keep for 3–4 days in an airtight container in the refrigerator. ❧ *Makes 600 g*

To make the salted-cod paste, soak the *baccalà* (available at specialist food stores) in fresh, cold water for 2–3 days, changing the water 5–6 times during this process. Drain and cut into 2.5 cm strips. Heat some olive oil in a large pot and fry the onion and garlic together. Add the strips of *baccalà* and toss well so that the *baccalà* is thoroughly coated. Add the bread, wine, parsley, pepper and cream and cook over a low heat for 20 minutes. Cool. Purée in a food processor, drizzling in the extra-virgin olive oil as required to form a smooth emulsification. Add a dash of verjuice to soften the flavour and texture. The paste will keep for 1 week in an airtight container in the refrigerator. ❧ *Makes 500 g*

Minestrone

Legend has it that monks invented minestrone and thus created the first restaurant. At the monastery a pot would go on in the morning and vegetables would be added as the day went on. Water was added as the pot dried, and its contents became a continuous 'restaurant' for weary travellers. ∾ From all accounts the Florentino is where many people had their first bowl of this vegetable brew. One famous story says that in the days when licensing rules allowed the consumption of only Australian wine at the restaurant, all the spirits, aperitifs and so on were kept in a box and stored in the boot of a waiter's car. When all the guests were settled in for their meal, the box would be delivered and the spoils dispersed. One lunchtime, during a raid by the licensing police and with the usual getaway route foiled, a quick-thinking member of staff emptied the liquor into the minestrone simmering on the stovetop. Apparently it was the best batch of minestrone ever. What would the monks have said? ∾ My minestrone recipe is simple, and the simplest of things need to be observed when making it: your ingredients must be first class, the *soffritto* must have time to caramelise and impart all those delicious sweet flavours, and you must season early. ∾ *Soffritto* (meaning 'lightly fried') is the basis for all our sauces and soups. It contains garlic, onions, carrots and celery, depending on the dish, and is essential in the *cucina*. It must be timed to fry slowly and well enough to allow the ingredients' natural sugars to caramelise, which produces a magnificent sweetness of smell and palate. Timing is everything here – just remember to 'let the onions fry'. ∾ *Serves 6 very hungry people*

1 tablespoon olive oil

1 clove garlic, finely chopped

1 onion, finely chopped

½ cup speck pieces

1 carrot, diced

1 turnip, peeled and diced

1 stalk celery, diced

1 teaspoon freshly crushed basil

pinch of dried oregano

1 cup dried borlotti beans, soaked overnight

¼ cabbage, chopped

3 stalks silver beet, diced

1 medium Spunta potato, peeled and diced

250 g pumpkin, peeled and diced

1 medium sweet potato, peeled and diced

1 tablespoon tomato paste

approximately 8 litres water

1 tablespoon sea salt

pinch of freshly ground black pepper

1 zucchini, diced

100 g green beans, sliced

2 bay leaves

handful of freshly chopped flat-leaf parsley

1 × 330 g can Italian tomatoes, chopped

extra-virgin olive oil

pesto (see page 36)

freshly grated Parmigiano-Reggiano

Heat the olive oil in a large, heavy-based pot. To make the *soffritto*, sauté the garlic, onion and speck until translucent. Add the carrot, turnip and celery and continue to sauté, then add the basil and oregano. Add the drained borlotti beans, cabbage, silver beet, potato, pumpkin and sweet potato and stir until the vegetables begin to soften. Add the tomato paste and cook for a couple of minutes. Pour in enough water to cover the vegetables comfortably, and season with salt and pepper. Bring to the boil, then reduce the heat to a gentle simmer and cook for at least 1 hour until the borlotti beans are tender, skimming from time to time to remove any impurities.

Add the zucchini, green beans, bay leaves, parsley and tomato. Simmer for 20 minutes over a gentle to moderate heat until all the vegetables have cooked through. Serve drizzled with extra-virgin olive oil and garnished with a teaspoon of pesto and some Parmigiano-Reggiano.

Linguine con le vongole – Pasta with clams, chilli, garlic and olive oil

This type of pasta dish is extremely Italian in style, with clean, simple flavours. It relies, of course, on best-quality ingredients, but more than this, on skill in handling the *padella* – the frying pan. Many Italian classics rely on quick, masterly handling of this utensil, never allowing it to smoke, as this destroys the dish, and making sure the food fries, not stews. If either of these things happen, the only solution is to start again. ∾ Make sure you trust your fishmonger. Buy fresh, live clams and when you get them home put them in a bucket of cold water and let them open. Use within 24 hours. Lift them out gently; any sand should fall to the bottom of the bucket. They need to drain well, because water and a hot pan do not mix – as you will quickly learn. ∾ *Serves 4*

400 g homemade linguine (or Rustichella brand, if making your own is not possible)

olive oil

1 clove garlic, finely chopped

1 chilli, seeded and finely sliced

1 teaspoon freshly crushed basil

sea salt and freshly cracked black pepper

4 handfuls of clams, rinsed and well drained

1 glass dry white wine

2 tablespoons freshly chopped flat-leaf parsley

Cook the pasta in a pot of boiling salted water. Drain thoroughly and keep warm. Heat 4 tablespoons olive oil in a frying pan that is large enough to accommodate all the ingredients at once. Add the garlic, chilli, basil and a little salt and pepper. Sauté, tossing well. Add the clams, which should sizzle but not smoke. Toss and cook for 2 minutes. Add the wine and cook for a further 1–2 minutes until all the clams have opened – the wine will disperse quite quickly due to the heat. Add the pasta. Drizzle over a little more olive oil and sprinkle with the parsley. Incorporate well by tossing for another minute or two over the heat. Serve immediately.

Rigatoni con verdure arrosto – Pasta with roasted vegetables

Simplicity and freshness are the essence of this dish, with a surprising depth of flavour provided by the initial roasting of the vegetables. It is a delight during any season, highlighting the produce of the day. You can alter the ingredients according to what is available. ∿ *Serves 8*

200 ml olive oil

4 cloves garlic, peeled

250 g pumpkin, peeled and roughly chopped

2 medium sweet potatoes, peeled and roughly chopped

1 parsnip, peeled and roughly chopped

3 zucchini, roughly chopped

2 sprigs rosemary

10 sage leaves

sea salt and freshly ground black pepper

1 kg rigatoni pasta

freshly chopped flat-leaf parsley

freshly grated Parmigiano-Reggiano

Preheat the oven to 180°C. Put the olive oil and garlic in a large baking tray, then add the vegetables. Roughly chop the rosemary and sage together and scatter over the vegetables. Season well, then toss everything gently with your hands until the vegetables are well coated with oil and herbs. Bake for 30 minutes or until soft.

Cook the rigatoni in a pot of boiling salted water until al dente. Drain. Toss the pasta through the baked vegetables, add some parsley and Parmigiano-Reggiano, and serve.

Tagliarini al pesto – Tagliarini with basil pesto

The smell of fresh basil in the air reminds me of eating outside at night, under my father's grapevines. When you make pesto the traditional way with the mortar and pestle, everybody knows about it! Apart from the wonderful sweet aroma, anyone nearby has to put up with the noise. I love to get green spots all over me as I go for another grind – it's great sport. A blender is a quick and easy option but it isn't as much fun – the friction dulls the flavour and your pesto won't be as *casalinga*. A pestle and mortar also extracts more juice from the basil. ∿ Pesto is a versatile dressing that can be used as a simple sauce or as an ingredient in many other dishes. For the best flavour and colour, use only the freshest ingredients, especially the basil. This recipe makes easily enough to dress 12 serves of pasta. Any left over can be stored in the refrigerator for 2 weeks in a screwtop jar with a film of oil to cover. ∿ *Serves 12*

200 g basil leaves

2 cloves garlic

100 g pine nuts

100 g freshly grated Parmigiano-Reggiano

100 g freshly grated pecorino

sea salt and freshly ground black pepper

350 ml good-quality olive oil

500 g homemade tagliarini (see page 217)

Using a large mortar and pestle, crush together all the ingredients except the olive oil and pasta. Blend in the olive oil gradually to form an emulsified paste, adding only a small amount of oil to begin with, just to get the dry ingredients to move. As you work, continually scrape the mixture from the sides into the centre of the bowl.

Cook the pasta in boiling salted water until al dente. Drain. Dress with pesto to taste and serve immediately.

Penne con pollo e piselli – Penne with smoked chicken and peas

I have known Tom Cooper, who specialises in smoked products, for many years. He is well known in the restaurant industry and does amazing things with a smoker oven. He will attempt almost anything and is very meticulous. For Grossi Florentino he smokes swordfish, and we also use his sensational salmon. When a side of Tom's smoked salmon arrives, I like to send the whole thing into the restaurant to be freshly sliced. I created this pasta dish for the Cellar Bar to showcase Tom's smoked chicken. Its flavour works really well with fresh peas. ～ *Serves 6*

olive oil

300 g Tom Cooper's smoked chicken, cut into small pieces

2 cloves garlic, finely chopped

1 onion, finely chopped

4 sage leaves, chopped

2 teaspoons pesto (see page 36)

100 ml white wine

400 ml chicken stock (see page 215)

400 ml cream

sea salt and freshly ground black pepper

150 g fresh peas, blanched in boiling water for 3 minutes

500 g penne pasta (preferably Martelli)

freshly grated Parmigiano-Reggiano

Put a little olive oil in a pan and sauté the smoked chicken pieces until golden. Set aside. In another pan, sauté the garlic and onion in a little olive oil until the onion is translucent. Stir in the sage and pesto, then add the wine and reduce by half. Stir in the chicken stock, cream and sautéed chicken, season to taste, and simmer for approximately 20 minutes until the chicken is well braised and the sauce reaches your desired consistency. Add the peas to the sauce and cook for a further 5 minutes. Meanwhile, cook the pasta in boiling salted water until al dente. Drain. Toss the pasta with the sauce, add some Parmigiano-Reggiano and serve.

Lasagne

It's comforting to know you can always get real lasagne in the Cellar Bar. This is my mother's recipe and at Grossi Florentino we try to make it exactly as she does. In the Cellar Bar, lasagne is served as an entrée and bread is always on the table. If you wish to make it into a meal on its own, serve it with a green salad. ◦ *Serves 4 as an entrée*

lasagne sheets

1 litre béchamel sauce (see page 214)

250 g freshly grated Parmigiano-Reggiano

SUGO BOLOGNESE

50 ml olive oil

1 large onion, finely chopped

2 cloves garlic, finely chopped

800 g minced beef

100 g minced pork

100 g minced chicken

1 tablespoon freshly chopped sage

1 tablespoon chopped oregano

1 bay leaf

2 cloves, crushed

a grating of nutmeg

sea salt and freshly ground black pepper

200 g tomato paste

200 ml red wine

2 litres beef stock (see page 216)

To make the *sugo bolognese*, heat the olive oil in a large pot and sauté the onion and garlic over medium heat for 4–5 minutes until soft and golden. Add all the meat and sauté for 10 minutes, stirring continuously, until well browned. Stir in the herbs and spices and season with salt and pepper. Add the tomato paste and cook for 1–2 minutes, then pour in the wine and boil to reduce by half. Add the beef stock and mix well. Bring to the boil, then reduce the heat and simmer gently for 1 hour.

When the *sugo bolognese* is ready, cook the lasagne sheets in boiling salted water until al dente. Drain and put into a bowl of cool water with a few drops of olive oil to prevent the sheets from sticking together. Preheat the oven to 180ºC.

Ladle a small amount of both sauces into an ovenproof tray. Cover with a layer of pasta. Ladle some more *sugo* over the pasta and drizzle over some béchamel sauce, then sprinkle with cheese. Continue to layer in this way until you reach the top of the tray, finishing with a layer of Parmigiano-Reggiano. Bake for 30 minutes.

Serve with a little extra *sugo*, if necessary, and more grated Parmigiano-Reggiano, if desired.

Insalata caprese – Tomato, basil and buffalo-milk mozzarella salad

When I visit Italy one of the first things I do is find a place where I can sit and have some bread, some local salami and a piece of buffalo-milk mozzarella. If you drizzle a great oil and a little salt and pepper on the cheese you can enjoy yourself for hours. ∾ This is one of the most popular salads I can think of. It combines ingredients that collectively epitomise the 'Italian thing' better than anything else. Try to find really good, flavoursome tomatoes – preferably ones that have been grown in the soil rather than hydroponically. Fruit grown in the soil must work to survive, and tastes much better as a result.

vine-ripened tomatoes, finely sliced

buffalo-milk mozzarella, finely sliced

basil leaves

red onion, finely diced

good-quality white-wine vinegar

extra-virgin olive oil

sea salt and freshly ground black pepper

baby capers

dried oregano

To assemble the salad, lay slices of tomato on a flat serving dish. Lay a slice of mozzarella on each slice of tomato, then a basil leaf on each mozzarella slice. Allow each ingredient to be visible so as to create a red, white and green effect. Continue until all the tomato, cheese and basil have been used. Sprinkle some onion down the centre of the salad and dress with vinegar and olive oil. Sprinkle with salt, pepper, capers and oregano and serve.

Spezzatino di manzo alla Toscana – Braised Tuscan-style beef with red wine, served with polenta

Nothing could be more comforting than this full-flavoured, Tuscan-style casserole. The mere smell of it cooking makes you feel at home and at ease. Coupled with polenta, the dish becomes a heart-warming feast. ～ *Serves 8*

olive oil

2 kg gravy beef, cut into large cubes

2 cloves garlic, chopped

2 onions, sliced

3 tablespoons tomato paste

pinch of freshly chopped rosemary

3–4 sage leaves, chopped

pinch of freshly grated nutmeg

3 cloves, crushed

500 ml full-bodied red wine

chilli (fresh or powdered) *or* paprika

pinch of salt and freshly ground black pepper

4 litres beef stock (see page 216)

2 litres water

500 g instant polenta

freshly grated Parmigiano-Reggiano (optional)

knob of butter (optional)

Heat some olive oil in a heavy-based pan and brown the beef well. In a separate, large pan, heat a little more oil and sauté the garlic. When it begins to colour, add the onion and sauté until golden. Add the tomato paste to this *soffritto* and cook until it caramelises. Add the rosemary, sage, nutmeg and cloves, mix the beef through and pour in the wine. Reduce for approximately 5 minutes. Add the chilli, salt and pepper to taste. Cover with the stock and simmer gently for at least 1–1½ hours, until the meat is tender.

Bring the water to a boil in a large, heavy-based pot and add salt. Pour in the polenta and cook gently for 3–5 minutes, stirring continuously, until the water has been absorbed. Flavour with Parmigiano-Reggiano and butter, if desired.

Serve the beef with plenty of polenta to mop up the juices. The casserole is even better reheated and served the next day.

Vitello tonnato – Thin slices of poached veal with tuna sauce

Vitello tonnato is one of the great classics of the *cucina italiana*. The recipe has been contorted in many ways but when it is made well, the flavours and textures are divine and it's a real crowd-pleaser. Here is our version, which is not dissimilar to that of Pellegrino Artusi (1820–1911), author of Italy's most renowned cookbook, *The Art of Eating Well*. I like to use hard-boiled egg in the sauce to add extra body and texture. My daughter, Loredana, is a vitello tonnato aficionado, so she always lets me know if the taste and texture are not up to scratch! ❧ *Serves 4–6 as an entrée*

olive oil

3 topsides or girello of young veal,
trimmed of all sinew

250 ml white wine

250 ml white vinegar

2 stalks celery, roughly chopped

3–4 cloves

3–4 juniper berries

2 bay leaves

sea salt and freshly ground black pepper

4 anchovies

TUNA SAUCE

500 g tinned tuna (preferably Ortiz)

100 g baby capers

5 hard-boiled eggs, finely grated

juice of 1 lemon

extra-virgin olive oil

reduction from the veal (see method)

sea salt and freshly ground black pepper

GARNISH

16–24 baby capers

shards of Parmigiano-Reggiano

8–12 lemon wedges

12–18 rocket leaves

freshly chopped flat-leaf parsley

Heat a little olive oil in a frying pan and sear the veal on both sides until lightly golden. Put the meat into a pot that is just large enough to fit all the ingredients. Add the wine, vinegar, celery, spices and bay leaves. Season, then pour in water to cover. Bring to a boil and simmer until the veal is just cooked, approximately 15 minutes. Remove a piece of meat from the liquid with a slotted spoon and poke it with a skewer – if the juices run clear, it is ready. If not, return to the pot and cook for a few more minutes. Do not overcook or the meat will be too dry. Remove the meat with a slotted spoon, then add the anchovies to the liquid and reduce by half. Strain the reduction through a fine sieve and allow to cool.

To make the sauce, purée the tuna in a blender, then add the capers, egg and lemon juice. With the machine going, slowly add a little olive oil. Still with the machine going, slowly add the cooled veal reduction until the mixture reaches a sauce-like consistency that will coat the veal.

Slice the veal as finely as you can. Spread half the tuna sauce in a serving dish and cover with the veal slices, then spread with the remaining sauce. Refrigerate overnight. Garnish each serve with 4 baby capers, some Parmigiano-Reggiano, 2 lemon wedges, 3 rocket leaves and a sprinkle of parsley.

47

La trippa stufata con pinoli e uvetta – Ox tripe slowly cooked with tomato and white wine, finished with pine nuts and muscatels

Tripe is one of those love–hate things. I once had tripe at Cecchino, a little restaurant situated next to an old abattoir outside Rome, which has built its name on cooking offal. Tripe is one of its specialities, along with oxtail and calf's feet dishes. Mmm – heaven! ∾ Tripe has been in the Italian repertoire for centuries. The Romans claim they have the best version, but I believe the Florentines do a great job with it, too. This is the way my dad taught me to cook it, and if you like tripe, you will love this. Make sure you use honeycomb tripe that has been precooked by the butcher or blanched by you at home. (Most tripe sold in Australia is precooked. If not, cut it into strips and simmer in salted water for 1 hour, then drain well.) ∾ *Serves 6*

1 tablespoon olive oil

1 clove garlic, finely chopped

1 onion, finely chopped

1 large carrot, cut into small batons

2 stalks celery, cut into small batons

4 cloves, crushed

½ teaspoon freshly grated nutmeg

1 chilli, seeded and finely chopped

1 teaspoon pesto (see page 36)

generous handful of freshly chopped flat-leaf parsley

sea salt and freshly ground black pepper

1 tablespoon tomato paste

1 kg honeycomb ox tripe (cooked), cut into thin strips

250 ml white wine

2 litres water *or* chicken stock (see page 215)

200 g dried muscatels

200 g pine nuts

freshly grated Parmigiano-Reggiano

Heat the olive oil in a deep pot, then add the garlic and onion and fry until translucent. Add the carrot and celery and cook well together for about 5 minutes. Stir in the spices, chilli, pesto and parsley. Season to taste with salt and pepper. Add the tomato paste and stir constantly until it has caramelised. Stir the tripe through. Pour in the wine and reduce slightly, stirring to mix well. Add enough water or stock to cover the tripe and cook on a low heat for 1 hour. Add the muscatels and pine nuts and simmer for a further 10 minutes. Serve scattered with a little extra parsley and some Parmigiano-Reggiano.

La Strada

Italian immigrants have not only improved what we eat in Australia, but how we eat it. Mediterranean cultures embrace the joys of street life and socialising out of doors, and gradually Australians have caught on.

We've always had the climate – what we needed was the attitude, which in Italy is all about the *bella figura*, that is, making a good impression. To do so requires being seen, whether out strolling or socialising over an al fresco meal, taking an *aperativo* at the bar, or grabbing an early-morning coffee by the curb. Italians live and socialise on the street (*la strada*), probably more than they do at home, and the neighbourhood bar and restaurant are the centres of community life: old friends meet by chance, girl meets boy, gossip is exchanged, arguments are sparked and settled.

The cafe in front of the Grill and Cellar Bar was one of Melbourne's first outdoor venues, adding another casual dining option to the business, and providing an entertaining outlook from the sought-after window seats within, whether on tourists posing for photographs amid the passing parade or on chance encounters.

Occasionally patrons inside are rewarded with more unusual antics, such as the vision of a former *Vogue* editor rearranging her appearance in full view: once, mistaking the Cellar Bar window for tinted glass in the early evening light, Sheila Scotter, Australia's style doyenne, stopped to deal with an untucked blouse. Turning her back to Bourke Street, she quickly hitched up her skirt and tugged down the offending garment, to the huge amusement of those inside, who were soon outside applauding her performance.

Philip Jones and his various Labradors have graced Florentino's footpath for so long that he was one of the favoured few given table service when, in the pre-Grossi era, others had to hand their order in at the bar. He has had many chance encounters, such as running into historian Manning Clark, who happened by one lunchtime in the mid-1970s. Stopping for a chat, Clark recounted a recent conversation with Sir Sidney Nolan's wife, Cynthia, who had told Clark she had decided she'd wasted her life with Nolan. A few months later she committed suicide.

As the proprietor with Sunday Reed (Cynthia Nolan's sister-in-law) of the East End Book Store in Exhibition Street, Jones was for many years a neighbour of the Florentino – the neighbours and the neighbourhood being an extension of *la strada*. Only Pellegrini's, the Job Warehouse, the Hill of Content bookshop, Mitty's newsagency, the Italian Waiter's Club and, of course, Grossi Florentino recall an area bounded by Bourke, Exhibition and Lonsdale streets and based around a cluster of Italian restaurants that once exemplified Melbourne's bohemian and intellectual life. The Molinas are long gone from the Imperial Hotel, and the Society, Ricco's, Mario's and the Latin (latterly Marchetti's Latin, owned by ex-Florentino employee Bill Marchetti) are no more.

Now an institution itself, Pellegrini's was started by two of Leon Massoni's favourite waiters, brothers Vildo and Lilliano Pellegrini. Leon recalls watching the building alterations under way on the corner of Crossley Lane and wondering what was up. A week before the 1956 Olympic Games began, he found out – when the Pellegrinis gave notice and then opened their coffee bar.

The flow of traffic between patrons of the Hill of Content and the adjoining Grossi Florentino is constant, a visit to one usually ensuring a stop at the other. Michael Zifcak used to run Collins Booksellers, which owns the bookshop and has its headquarters above it, but in retirement still retains his office on the other side of the Mural Room wall. In 1952, when Collins moved in, Zifcak looked at the Florentino's prices and decided he couldn't afford them. 'I was only the accountant then and was used to going to the Coles cafeteria,' he says. 'My first visit to Flo's was in about 1960 as the guest of a Scottish publisher. I was the new managing director by then and enormously pleased to be taken. He told me we owed them £342, an amount that had been outstanding since our founder was killed in an accident six months before, and he had come to collect it.'

Zifcak explained the circumstances to the Scotsman and said he didn't have the money, to which his host responded that he'd go after it. 'Can I explain how I pay the monthly accounts?' Zifcak replied. 'I put them all in a hat and get a bank statement. Then I draw out accounts until I've reached the overdraft limit. If you don't leave me alone, I won't even put you in the hat.' Having swallowed this tease, the publisher then agreed to Zifcak's usual

extended credit arrangement and they ended up the best of friends.

In the Tsindos years Zifcak began frequenting the Mural Room, where he entertained overseas publishers he wanted to impress, like Paul Hamlyn (who always signed his letters to Zifcak 'Cuddles'). 'Whenever I am invited to lunch I not only nominate the Florentino but insist on it. We have a regular book retailers' lunch that's always at the Florentino because I know I won't get cold, wet or caught in traffic and that I'm going to eat well. The others wanted to change to the Latin at one stage but I wouldn't have it and persuaded them to stay. I've picked up a cappuccino next door every morning for twenty-two years. There's a wonderful sense of friendship, neighbourliness and belonging.'

Even after he left the Florentino, George Tsindos remained a neighbourhood figure. He still lived around the corner in Spring Street, collecting his daily papers from Mitty's as he had done for forty-five years and keeping an eagle eye on the comings and goings at the Bourke Street restaurants. 'We've all been here so long and we all know each other,' says Carmel Dwyer of Mitty's. 'From Spring Street to Exhibition Street, it's like a family.'

Or like an Italian main square where no one misses a trick, whether it's VIPs arriving at the Florentino on Cup Eve or a bride at the sidewalk cafe with her feet up, puffing on a cigarette before striking another sophisticated pose in the Restaurant doorway.

53

Diplomatica

Simple ingredients assembled with care make this traditional Italian cake a must for our Cellar Bar. The freshness of the cream is a backdrop to the sweetness of the jam, and it is all given life with the crunch of the pastry. ∾ *Serves 12*

3 × 28 cm × 21 cm puff pastry sheets
(see page 218)

500 ml cream, whipped

500 ml pastry cream (see page 219)

500 g strawberry *or* raspberry conserve

Preheat the oven to 180°C. Put the sheets of puff pastry on a greased tray with another tray on top to weigh them down. Bake for 20 minutes until golden brown. Remove from the oven and allow to cool.

Fold the whipped cream into the pastry cream until blended. Put a sheet of puff pastry on a large, flat serving dish. Cover completely with a thick layer of conserve and then a thick layer of cream. Repeat the process until all the ingredients have been used, finishing with a layer of cream. Lightly draw a fork across the cream to create a wave pattern. Smooth the sides with a spatula. Refrigerate for 2 hours.

Using a very sharp serrated knife, carefully cut the cake into 7 cm squares – work with a sawing motion, without pressing down. Serve immediately.

Cannoli alla siciliana

There are few sweet treats more typically Sicilian than *cannoli*. The flaky tube-shaped pastries share their fame with *cassata*, another sweet Sicilian classic. The pastry is wrapped around a cylinder (or '*cannoli* form', available at specialist kitchenware stores), and then fried. In times past, this cylinder was made of cane, or *canna* in Italian – hence the name *cannoli*. ᨒ What you fill your *cannoli* with is only limited by your imagination, but tradition dictates that ricotta must be part of the filling. ᨒ *Makes 12*

4 tablespoons butter

380 g flour

1 egg

2 egg yolks

125 ml marsala

vegetable oil *or* cottonseed oil

icing sugar

CANNOLI FILLING

300 g fresh ricotta

200 g mascarpone

caster sugar

handful of fruit and nuts (including candied peel, clementines, glacé cherries, blanched almonds)

maraschino liqueur

Rub the butter into the flour until well combined. Add the egg, egg yolks and marsala and knead to a dough. Refrigerate for 30 minutes before rolling out thinly on a floured surface. Cut 10 cm squares of dough and wrap the squares around *cannoli* forms. Deep-fry for about 30 seconds in hot oil in a deep pan or wok, moving the forms around with a slotted spoon. Do not crowd the pan. Using tongs, gently lift each *cannoli* shell from the oil and, with a second set of tongs, tap the form so that it falls out. Return the shell to the oil for 30 seconds to cook the inside. Drain on paper towel and allow to cool.

To make the filling, blend the ricotta, mascarpone and caster sugar until they form a smooth paste. Finely chop the candied peel, clementines (see page 212) and cherries. Toast the almonds until golden brown, then chop them. Transfer the blended cheese into a large bowl and add the chopped fruit and nuts, and maraschino to taste. Gently mix until well incorporated. Pipe the filling into the cooled *cannoli* shells and stack them up on a serving dish. Sprinkle generously with icing sugar – they will look sensational.

NOTE: To transform *cannoli* from an afternoon snack to an elegant dessert, serve with a blood-orange sorbet.

Zeppole di San Giuseppe – Sweet dumplings rolled in sugar

The desserts from the south of Italy are fantastic, and you see delicious doughnut-shaped *zeppole* in every *pasticceria*. They are traditionally made to celebrate the feast of San Giuseppe. This recipe comes from my sister-in-law, Marisa, who is of Neapolitan descent. ❧ *Makes 10*

30 g fresh yeast

500 g potatoes, peeled

500 g flour

50 g softened butter

1 tablespoon caster sugar

4 eggs

vegetable oil *or* cottonseed oil

extra caster sugar

Dissolve the yeast in a little warm water. Boil the potatoes until soft, then drain. Mash or put through a potato ricer while still warm. Put the flour in a large bowl and make a well in the centre. Put the mashed potato into the well with the butter, sugar and yeast. Mix to form a firm dough. Add the eggs one at a time, incorporating each one well before adding the next. (This can be done in an electric mixer, using the paddle attachment.)

Roll out the dough on a floured surface to approximately 1 cm thick. Using a circular cutter 8 cm in diameter, cut rounds from the dough. With a smaller cutter, cut out the centre from the rounds. Put the hollow rounds on a tray and allow to prove in a warm spot for 10 minutes.

In hot oil in a deep pan or wok, deep-fry 3–4 *zeppole* at a time for 3–4 minutes until golden, moving them around with a slotted spoon. Do not crowd the pan. Remove from the oil and immediately roll in caster sugar. Serve warm or cold on the day you make them.

Torta di limone – Lemon tart

I don't know anyone who isn't partial to a slice of lemon tart. I adopted this recipe years ago and stuck to it. It is rustic and rich, yet very clean on the palate as it is loaded with acid. It takes time to make. ∾ After you have cooked the tart, allow it to cool completely but do not refrigerate it – at room temperature the texture of the filling is deliciously soft and the pastry remains short and brittle.

9 eggs

grated zest and juice of 4 lemons

375 g caster sugar

300 ml cream, whipped

LEMON PASTRY

500 g unsalted butter

1 kg flour

650 g caster sugar

2 eggs

1 egg yolk

pinch of salt

grated zest of 2 lemons

egg wash (1 egg whisked with a pinch of salt)

To make the pastry, rub the butter into the flour until the mixture resembles breadcrumbs. In a separate bowl, whisk the sugar with the eggs and yolk. Add the salt and lemon zest, then blend in the sugar/egg mixture. Do not overwork. Refrigerate for 30 minutes before use. (The quantities given here make enough for 3 tart bases. Any unused dough can be frozen for later use.)

Preheat the oven to 200°C. Grease a 24 cm × 5 cm deep springform tin. Roll out the dough to a thickness of 5 mm and line the tin carefully with the pastry, levelling off the top with a sharp knife. Patch any small holes with pieces of cut-off dough. Refrigerate for 15 minutes. Line the pastry with aluminium foil and fill with rice or dried beans. Blind-bake for 15 minutes. Remove from the oven, gently lift out the weights and foil, and brush the pastry with the egg wash. Return to the oven for 3–4 minutes until the egg has set – this will seal the tart case completely. Reduce the oven temperature to 150°C.

Whisk the eggs, then add the zest, juice and sugar and whisk until well combined. Fold the cream through the egg and lemon mixture. Pour the filling into the tart case and bake for 1½ hours on the bottom shelf of the oven until just set – touch the surface lightly with your finger to check. Allow to cool for a few hours and serve at room temperature. The tart does not need any accompaniment, although a little clotted cream can work well.

Torta di cioccolato e pera – Chocolate pear tart

Chocolate and pear – what a great combination, and this tart really makes it work. The freshness of the fruit bites through the chocolate like a razor. ∾ This northern-inspired dessert is great hot or cold and never seems to last very long, as it is so popular. I like to use Corella pears, but there are many varieties to choose from – you will find your favourite. Always use high-quality chocolate.

100 g dark chocolate (preferably Valrhona)

50 g unsalted butter

1 tablespoon orange marmalade

2 ripe pears

2 eggs, separated

100 g caster sugar

CHOCOLATE PASTRY

50 g unsalted butter

100 g plain flour

30 g cocoa powder

50 g caster sugar

1 egg, lightly beaten

To make the pastry, rub the butter into the flour until the mixture resembles breadcrumbs. Sift in the cocoa powder and add the sugar, then add enough of the egg to bind the mixture together. Turn out onto your workbench and knead lightly. Wrap in plastic wrap and chill for 20 minutes.

Melt the chocolate and butter together in a saucepan over a low heat. Cool. Preheat the oven to 180°C. Grease a 28 cm fluted flan tin.

Roll out the dough to a thickness of 5 mm on a floured surface. Lightly press the dough into the flan tin, then brush with the marmalade. Peel and core the pears, cut into quarters and arrange in the pastry shell.

Beat the egg yolks and sugar until pale and fluffy, then fold in the cooled chocolate mixture. Whisk the egg whites until stiff and fold into the mixture. Pour over the pears and bake for 40 minutes until the filling has firmed slightly and the pears have softened. Don't panic if the filling seems too runny – it will firm up as the tart cools a little. Serve warm or cold, with cream.

Torta di pinoli – Pine-nut tart

What an attractive way to use pine nuts – the finished tart looks like a mosaic in a Roman ruin. It is simple but effective, keeps well and tastes as good as it looks.

60 g sultanas

60 ml brandy

120 g softened butter

100 g icing sugar

100 g ground almonds

1 egg

75 g clementines (see page 212), chopped

100 g glacé cherries, chopped

120 g pine nuts

TART PASTRY

1 kg flour

pinch of salt

500 g unsalted butter

650 g caster sugar

2 eggs

1 egg yolk

Put the sultanas in the brandy to soak. To make the pastry, sift the flour and salt, then rub the butter in until the mixture resembles breadcrumbs. In a separate bowl, whisk together the sugar, eggs and egg yolk. Blend with the flour/butter mixture, but do not overwork. Refrigerate for 30 minutes before use. (The quantities given here make enough for 3 tart bases. Any unused dough can be frozen for later use.)

Preheat the oven to 200°C. Grease a 28 cm fluted flan tin. In a large bowl, combine the butter, icing sugar and ground almonds. Add the egg and mix until well combined. Fold in the clementines, the cherries and the sultanas with their soaking liquid.

Roll out the dough on a floured surface to approximately 5 mm thick and press into the prepared tin. Line with a sheet of greaseproof paper and fill with rice or dried beans. Blind-bake for 20 minutes. Remove from the oven, gently lift out the weights and paper and allow to cool. Reduce the oven temperature to 170°C.

Pour the filling into the cooled tart shell and sprinkle the pine nuts over evenly. Gently press the pine nuts into the filling with the back of a spoon. Bake for 15–20 minutes or until golden brown. Allow to cool completely before removing from the tin (if you don't do this, the tart will break). Serve with cream.

Torta di cioccolato bianco e formaggio –
White-chocolate cheesecake

There is a vast number of recipes in the Italian repertoire for baked cheesecake, from the rustic Neapolitan ricotta torte to the more delicate versions of the northern regions. I particularly like this one because it is very simple to make.

160 g white chocolate (preferably Valrhona)

650 g cream cheese, softened

250 g caster sugar

3 eggs, lightly beaten

grated zest and juice of 1 orange

seeds from ½ vanilla bean

200 g raspberries

icing sugar

Preheat the oven to 160°C. Lightly grease a 5 cm deep, rectangular baking dish (28 cm × 21 cm) and line it with greaseproof paper.

Melt the white chocolate in a double boiler until smooth. Combine the cream cheese and sugar, then slowly add the melted chocolate, eggs, orange zest and juice, and vanilla seeds. Pour half the mixture into the baking dish. Cover with the raspberries and pour over the remaining mixture. Bake for 1 hour until just set. Allow to cool – the cake will become more stable and easier to cut. Dust with icing sugar and serve warm or at room temperature from the paper-lined dish.

Biscotti

For some reason the *biscotti* section of the *pasticceria* window catches my eye before anything else. I believe *biscotti* typify Italian *dolci*, or sweets, and to see them made with care is a sign of loving hands and a good home. Following are three of my favourite *biscotti* recipes. ❧ Florentines typify the more extravagant *cucina italiana*; the use of honey, almonds, chocolate and other luxury ingredients reflects the craftsmanship of Caterina de'Medici's brigade of chefs, which she took to the French court with her from Florence. She brought many other Italian delicacies to France, including macaroons and *frangipane*. ❧ *Biscotti di mandorle*, in contrast to Florentines, are a simple, pleasing biscuit of Sicilian origin. They are difficult to resist – especially served with a glass of Malvasia! ❧ The revolutionary leader Giuseppe Garibaldi, with his Thousand Men, reunited Italy by taking Sicily from the Bourbons in the mid-nineteenth century. It is said that he instructed his cook to produce a long-keeping foodstuff for his armies to eat while on the march. The Garibaldi biscuit was the result.

FLORENTINES

50 g unsalted butter

100 g cream

150 g caster sugar

40 g honey

35 g liquid glucose

135 g almond flakes

120 g hazelnuts, finely chopped

75 g candied orange peel, finely chopped

75 g glacé cherries, chopped

250 g dark chocolate (preferably Valrhona)

To make the Florentines, preheat the oven to 160°C and grease 2 large baking sheets. Bring the butter, cream and sugar to the boil in a saucepan. When the mixture has turned a golden caramel colour, add the honey and glucose and remove from the heat. Combine the nuts and fruit in a bowl. Add the caramel mixture and stir until evenly mixed. Spoon tablespoonfuls onto the prepared tray and flatten each Florentine with the back of the spoon. Bake for 10–12 minutes – the biscuits will bubble a little but will not change much in appearance. Leave to cool on the baking sheets. Melt the chocolate in a double boiler. Turn the cooled biscuits over and put a spoonful of chocolate on each. Spread and smooth the chocolate with a spatula. If you like, run a fork through the chocolate to create a wavy pattern. Allow to cool and harden. The biscuits will keep for 1 week in an airtight container. There is no need to refrigerate them. ❧ *Makes 40*

BISCOTTI DI MANDORLE (ALMOND BISCUITS)

250 g icing sugar

250 g ground almonds

1–2 egg whites, lightly beaten

30 glacé cherries

GARIBALDI BISCUITS

300 g unsalted butter

400 g flour, sifted

150 g caster sugar

400 g currants

4 egg whites, lightly beaten

extra caster sugar

To make the almond biscuits, preheat the oven to 160°C. Thoroughly grease and flour 2 large baking sheets. Combine the icing sugar and ground almonds in a bowl, then add the egg whites, mixing to form a paste. Using a pastry bag fitted with a star nozzle, pipe small amounts of paste, about the size of a 50-cent piece and 2.5 cm high, onto the prepared sheets. Push a glacé cherry into each biscuit. Bake for 10–12 minutes until firm to the touch but not coloured. Allow to cool on the baking sheets. The biscuits will keep for 1 week in an airtight container. ❧ *Makes 30*

To make the Garibaldi biscuits, preheat the oven to 160°C. Line a large baking sheet with greaseproof paper. Rub the butter into the flour until the mixture resembles breadcrumbs. Stir in the sugar and currants, then add most of the beaten egg white and mix to form a soft, but not sticky, dough. Using a spatula, spread the dough onto the baking sheet to a thickness of 2 cm. Flatten with the back of a spoon or a spatula that has been dipped in water (to stop the utensil sticking to the dough). Brush the dough with the remaining egg white and sprinkle with a little sugar. Bake for 15 minutes or until golden. Remove to a wire rack and allow to cool. Using a sharp knife, cut into fingers. The biscuits will keep for 1 week in an airtight container. ❧ *Makes 30–40*

The Grill

The Grill is Grossi Florentino's modern face. The epitome of sophisticated, contemporary dining Italian-style, its aim is to serve simple food based on fresh local ingredients, with slick, quick service.

When it opened as the Bistro Grill in 1959, however, this concept, now emulated and developed Australia-wide, was unknown. The Grill grew out of the success of Il Bistro (now the Cellar Bar) – and Australians' love of steak and chips. George Tsindos and Leon Massoni reckoned correctly that anything built around these ingredients and done well had to be successful. From day one the Bistro Grill was even more popular than Il Bistro, with people standing to eat behind those who were already seated at the long counter, or queuing into the street for the original eight tables.

In the beginning it was full of artists and university students, but, said George, they were soon followed by 'le tout Melbourne' once the then Lord Mayor's wife, Lady (Elvie) Curtis, decided she enjoyed the cosmopolitan scene. The menu was simple: minestrone, oysters, spaghetti bolognaise and spaghetti napoli, and one fish, two steaks and lamb chops, with a choice of scallop potatoes, ricotta croquettes or iceberg lettuce. Unlike Il Bistro, the Grill had a general restaurant licence, and the tipple of choice was Penfold's flagon or cask wine at one shilling (10 cents) a glass.

The Bistro Grill took shape under the Mural Room in what had been a shopfront, rented out as a second-hand shop to a woman who had then sublet it to a driving school. Renowned architect Roy Grounds, then in partnership with Robin Boyd and Frederick Romberg, commenced the renovation but soon after left the group to work on the new arts centre planned for St Kilda Road. Boyd took over, but Grounds didn't lose interest in what was taking place – George would open the doors for the workmen at 8 a.m. and by 8.30, twice a week, Grounds would be there to look around. This happened for the length of the project.

More a bistro than a formal dining room, the original design was a long, narrow space in Boyd's distinctive style and colourings: burgundy leather banquettes along the west wall, matched by small, wine-coloured tessellated wall tiles, black chairs and white tabletops. A big copper canopy covered the flaming, open gas–charcoal grill, fronted by a counter and bar stools that ran the length of the room from the cash register just inside the door.

The Bistro Grill quickly became Melbourne's lifestyle hub, says Jonathon Crawford, an early devotee and leading member of the young social set in the 1960s. Every day he would wend his way from his clothing business in Flinders Lane, via the rear of the Oriental Hotel in Collins Street (where the ANZ Tower is now), to his reserved end table. There he would be joined for lunch by the likes of lingerie manufacturer John Gould, developer Cam Woolstencroft, model Jenny Ham, Georgina Weir, Dale Harper (later Lady Tryon and a friend of Prince Charles), solicitor Nicky Holt, stockbroker Peter Wenzel and entrepreneur Gary Van Egmond. Weir was studying but preferred the Bistro Grill – and the older men it attracted – to scruffy student pubs. She says it's where she learnt to drink wine (even though at first she laced it with lemonade), and that it was a gathering place for a whole group of people, including anyone who happened to be visiting from Sydney.

'They'd go straight to Flo's Grill because that's where you'd find anyone "happening" in Melbourne and discover what they were doing and where the parties were that night,' says Crawford. 'The spaghetti was always great, but the boys generally ate the char-grilled chops with scallop potatoes. There were two chefs behind the grill and you'd call instructions to them. George and Ray Tsindos were always there. They knew everyone by their first name and always had time to say hello.'

Raymond Tsindos remembers them well. He says all the young blades cut their teeth in Il Bistro and then moved on to the Bistro Grill, where they'd tip the girls behind the counter.

Sitting at the counter one evening, the ubiquitous Peter Rowland (who ate in some part of the Florentino seven or eight times a week) saved the Bistro and probably the building from burning down. The flue over the charcoal grill caught fire and all the other patrons fled. Notwithstanding the fact that he was wearing a beautiful suede

jacket, Rowland grabbed a fire extinguisher and put out the flames as the fire brigade smashed through the plate-glass front door. Rowland's jacket was ruined in the process and he asked George about a replacement, but George told him to claim it on his insurance. 'And this was *before* he barred me,' says Rowland (see page 136).

(see page 136)

'There weren't that many good restaurants around and it was the closest thing Melbourne had to a New York steakhouse, in the Bourke Street strip that also included the Society, Ricco's and Pellegrini's,' says Crawford. 'Everyone gravitated there, including the whole of Queen Street and William Street, where the barristers had offices. You'd see dozens of guys walking there and back every lunchtime.' Regulars phoned ahead to say they'd be arriving in ten minutes and wanted their steak on the plate and waiting on the counter when they walked in the door. If there was nowhere to sit, they'd stand to eat.

For a few years in the 1980s Kozminsky Jewellers, situated at the other end of Bourke Street, recognised the advantage of joining forces with another of the city's iconic institutions. The Grill had a display cabinet in the front window and a regularly changing array of Kozminsky's finest offerings appeared in it, a source of much interest to female patrons. Kurt Albrecht, Kozminsky's owner, dined upstairs most weeknights and many deals were done there. Ben, one of Albrecht's sons, recalls his father handing a five-carat diamond to a fellow diner and suggesting he take it home to his wife, which he did. She later handed it back, saying that because it was so big it didn't look real!

When Floyd Podgornik renovated the Florentino in 1989 he enlarged the Bistro Grill, doing away with the counter bar and its stools and provoking a mass exodus to the Cellar Bar. Even so, frequent diner Lindsay Fox would often put his head round the door and ask for his chops to be cooked a special way: burnt on the outside and raw within.

Ron Walker was and remains a fan of the Grill, which he favours on a regular basis over the Restaurant and the Cellar Bar. He says the Restaurant is for occasions such as lunches with the federal treasurer, Peter Costello, and businessman Peter Lowy. As Melbourne's Lord Mayor from 1974 to 1976, Walker dined at the Restaurant all the time, entertaining Henry and Nancy Kissinger on one occasion and, during a city

ABOVE Cellar master Peter Papini has been with the Grossi family for twenty years. Apart from compiling Grossi Florentino's wine lists with Guy, and ordering and buying the wine, he is a well-known fixture in the Cellar Bar where he works alongside Elda D'Amico.

garbage strike called by union leader John Halfpenny, being lectured by Malcolm Fraser on the evils of communism. The Grill is where he took former Victorian premier Jeff Kennett to cheer him up on the day his wife, Felicity, left him (they've since reunited). And you can forget all talk of the Liberal Party's plotting at the Melbourne Club – at least in recent times. 'That's nonsense. There was plenty of political planning and it was all done at the Florentino Grill,' says Walker, a former party treasurer and fundraiser. 'It was a house of intrigue during the decade we were in opposition [1983–96]: a lot of disappointed people gathered there and certain decisions were made that helped shape Australia.'

While he agrees that many people prefer the quieter, more well-spaced ambience of upstairs for such important conversations, Walker has a simple solution for ensuring privacy in the more cheek-by-jowl atmosphere of the Grill: he simply reserves the table next to him to make sure it stays empty. And while he enjoys the anonymity of reading a newspaper in the Cellar Bar, it was to the Grill that he hastened to return after his Hudson Conway business interests sold Crown Casino and its associated restaurants to the Packers. He also orders takeaway meals from the Grill, which are collected by taxi and taken to his home.

These days an extensive variety of dishes is served, but the regulars love the fact that the Grossis will cook off the menu for them. While the old set-up is still missed (not to mention the original Boyd design features), many regulars have become attached to the Grill's improved outlook onto Bourke Street and vie for the window seats, where they enjoy sitting and watching the world pass.

Peperoni arrosto al basilico – Oven-roasted capsicums marinated with fresh basil leaves

Antipasto means 'before the meal' and, like hors d'oeuvres, starters and savouries, *antipasti* are traditional offerings to stimulate the tastebuds. They are an opportunity to showcase the latest *salumi* (preserved meats), new season's vegetables, and the pantry's wares. My favourite *antipasti* recipes are too numerous to mention, but this recipe, and the four that follow, represent a selection. ∿ When capsicums are cooked as in this recipe their colour remains bright and they become very sweet. Persian fetta is a Yarra Valley cheese made to an old recipe and marinated in garlic, thyme and oil. It is a luscious, soft cheese, not too salty with a creamy texture, and marries well with the sweet roasted capsicum. Other cheeses can be used in this recipe, such as buffalo-milk mozzarella, for a very different texture. ∿ *Serves 4*

4 large red capsicums

sea salt and freshly ground black pepper

200 ml olive oil

4 cloves garlic, sliced

½ cup firmly packed basil leaves

100 g Yarra Valley Persian fetta, crumbled

extra-virgin olive oil

Opposite, clockwise from top: Duck terrine (page 84),
mussels topped with marinated eggplant (page 82),
fondue of fontina cheese (page 80),
grissini (page 152), honey-cured salmon (page 81),
oven-roasted capsicums (page 78).

Preheat the oven to 200°C. Put the capsicums in a baking tray and season with salt and pepper. Drizzle with some of the olive oil and bake for about 15 minutes, turning occasionally, until all the skin is very dark and the flesh has softened a little. Remove from the oven and quickly put into a large bowl. Cover tightly with plastic wrap so that no air escapes, and allow to cool. Remove the core from each capsicum and carefully peel off the skin, trying not to tear any of the flesh. Break open the flesh at one side so that you end up with a large strip. Discard the seeds and lay the capsicum flat in a ceramic dish. Sprinkle with the garlic and most of the basil leaves, reserving a few for the garnish. Season with salt and pepper and drizzle with the rest of the olive oil. Leave to marinate for about 2 hours. (If you are not planning to serve the dish on the same day, put the capsicums in the refrigerator.) To serve, scatter the reserved basil leaves and the fetta over the capsicum. Sprinkle with pepper and drizzle with extra-virgin olive oil.

Fonduta – Fondue of fontina cheese

This is a classic dish from Piemonte, the northern Italian region at the foot of the Alps, where dishes are typically made to provide warmth. Piemonte is noted for this *antipasto* fondue and for *bagna cauda*, a hot anchovy and garlic sauce. ❧ It is also famous for truffles, especially the pungent and flavoursome white truffles from Alba in the south-east (*tartufo bianco* or *tartufo d'Alba*). They are very rare and in Australia are only obtainable fresh if pre-ordered from specialist retailers, who usually sell them for upwards of $4000 a kilogram. Tinned truffles, which are generally high-quality French black truffles from Périgord, are more readily available (and cheaper). ❧ The traditional fondue pot is copper, lined with stainless steel, but any attractive stainless steel pot will suffice. ❧ *Serves 4*

50 ml milk

50 ml cream

1 bay leaf

100 g fontina cheese, chopped

sea salt and freshly ground black pepper

a grate of fresh nutmeg

1 fresh *or* tinned truffle, shaved (optional)

Put the milk, cream and bay leaf into a stainless steel pot and bring to simmering point. Whisk the cheese into the milk/cream mixture a little at a time. When all the cheese has melted, test the flavour and season with salt and pepper. Take off the heat, grate a little nutmeg over and top with truffle shavings, if using. Serve with olive *grissini* (see page 152) or *crostini* (page 217) for dipping.

Salmone stagionato – Honey-cured salmon

Whenever I'm in Rome I try to find time to dine at the famous fish restaurant La Rosetta, near the Pantheon. Chef Massimo Riccioli and his staff serve a wonderful array of seafood *antipasti*, often marinated with citrus, spices and salts. This recipe was inspired by my visits to La Rosetta. ∾ *Serves 8*

1 side (approximately 1.5 kg) Atlantic salmon

2 teaspoons freshly cracked black pepper

½ cup freshly chopped dill

10 juniper berries

4 star anise

4 cloves

185 g honey

185 g salt

½ cup watercress, picked into sprigs

extra-virgin olive oil

Lay the salmon skin-side down on your work surface. Using a small pair of pliers or tweezers, remove the bones that run through the flesh from the neck to the mid-section. (If you prefer, ask your fishmonger to 'pin-bone' the salmon when you purchase it.) Put the salmon in a deep glass or stainless steel dish, skin-side down, and sprinkle evenly with pepper and dill. Crush the juniper berries, star anise and cloves together and sprinkle over the fish. Cover with the honey and pack down with the salt. Cover with plastic wrap and refrigerate for 3 hours. Turn the fish, then refrigerate overnight.

To serve, slice very thinly and arrange the slices on a plate. Form the watercress sprigs into a nice bundle, put the bundle in the centre of the fish, and drizzle the whole with extra-virgin olive oil.

Cozze con caponata – Mussels topped with marinated eggplant

I love mussels, especially when they are still full of fresh seawater. On trips to the beach my dad used to scoop them out of their shells and eat them with a little olive oil and lemon juice. When I dine on mussels combined with wonderful *caponata* flavours, as described here, I feel like I'm in the Italian south. The Bay of Taranto in the far south is known for the best black mussels in Italy. ⤳ *Serves 4*

1 kg mussels, cleaned and bearded

1 clove garlic, finely chopped

150 ml white wine

sea salt and freshly ground black pepper

extra-virgin olive oil

CAPONATA

60 ml olive oil

1 small onion, finely diced

1 clove garlic, thinly sliced

1 stalk celery, finely diced

1 red capsicum, seeded and finely diced

300 ml vegetable oil

1 eggplant, cubed

100 ml vinegar

50 g black olives, pitted and chopped

50 g pine nuts, toasted

50 g sultanas *or* raisins

20 g sugar

½ cup finely chopped flat-leaf parsley

sea salt and freshly ground black pepper

To make the caponata, heat the olive oil and fry the onion and garlic until translucent. Add the celery and fry until it begins to soften, then add the capsicum and cook until tender. Transfer to a large bowl. Heat the vegetable oil in a separate pan and fry the eggplant until golden. Transfer to the bowl and stir. Add the vinegar, olives, pine nuts, sultanas, sugar and parsley, season with salt and pepper and toss well. Cover and allow to marinate for 3–4 hours before serving.

Warm a large, lidded pot over a medium–high heat. Put the mussels, garlic and white wine into the pot. Season with salt and pepper, cover and cook for 3–5 minutes or until all the shells have opened completely. Remove from the heat and allow to cool a little. Discard any shells that do not open. Lift the mussels from the pot (reserving the delicious juices for another use) and carefully break off and discard the empty half of each shell. Serve at room temperature on the half-shell, garnished with caponata and drizzled with extra-virgin olive oil.

Terrina di anatra – Duck terrine

I have a soft spot for terrines. The hard work of layering the meat and vegetables is rewarded when you slice through and watch your artistic design appear. ∽ A good poultry supplier will be able to advise you on the best duck legs. If you prefer to buy whole ducks and bone them yourself, you could roast the breasts and layer them in the terrine, or serve them as part of a second course with a great pinot noir. ∽ Firm Casteluccio lentils from Umbria are considered the best in Italy. They are available in Australia from specialist retailers such as Simon Johnson. ∽ *Serves 8–10*

1 onion, chopped

1 carrot, cut into batons

2 stalks celery, cut into batons

8 × 150 g duck legs

1 teaspoon ground star anise

1 teaspoon ground juniper berries

sea salt and freshly ground black pepper

1 sprig rosemary

1 bay leaf

2 cloves garlic, roughly chopped

1.5 litres duck fat (available from poultry suppliers), melted

1 cos lettuce

freshly chopped herbs (a mixture of chervil, dill, parsley, tarragon and coriander)

extra-virgin olive oil

balsamic vinegar (optional)

Preheat the oven to 160°C. Put the onion, carrot and celery in a deep baking tray, arrange the duck legs on top and sprinkle with the star anise and juniper. Season to taste, add the rosemary, bay leaf and garlic, and pour over the duck fat. Bake for about 1 hour or until the meat is falling off the bone.

Meanwhile, cook the lentils (ingredients opposite). Sauté the garlic, onion, carrot, celery and bay leaf in the olive oil until the vegetables are just tender. Add the lentils and stir-fry for 2 minutes. Pour in the stock, season with salt and pepper and simmer over a medium heat for 30 minutes until the lentils are just cooked. Allow to cool completely.

Drain and reserve the fat from the baking tray. Discard the rosemary, bay leaf and garlic cloves. Remove the skin from the duck legs and pull off the meat. Discard the bones and transfer the meat to a large bowl. Dice the baked carrot and celery and add to the bowl. Season with salt and pepper and mix well, adding a little of the reserved fat.

Blanch the cos leaves in boiling water and refresh in cold water. Line a 30 cm × 6 cm × 6 cm terrine mould with plastic wrap and then line it with

BRAISED LENTILS

1 clove garlic, finely diced

½ onion, finely diced

½ carrot, finely diced

1 stalk celery, finely diced

1 bay leaf

50 ml olive oil

100 g black lentils (preferably Casteluccio)

500 ml chicken stock (see page 215)

sea salt and freshly ground black pepper

cos leaves so that when you fill the mould, you will be able to wrap the leaves over the top. Gently squash half the duck mixture into the mould. Make a 2 cm deep trench in the centre of the meat and fill with lentils (you will have some left over – reserve them). Add the rest of the meat and press down firmly. Wrap the cos leaves over the top and cover tightly with plastic wrap. Weight the terrine with a milk carton to help it keep its shape, and refrigerate.

To serve, put a small pile of reserved lentils in the centre of each plate. Cut a 1 cm slice from the terrine and lay it gently on top of the lentils. Scatter with fresh herbs and drizzle with extra-virgin olive oil. Drizzle some oil around the plate, too, and add a splash of balsamic vinegar, if desired.

Fettuccine all'aragosta – Pasta ribbons with rock lobster and vermouth sauce

Whenever this dish is on our menu it is so popular we watch it walk out the door! Homemade pasta with lobster and other tasty things tossed through it – what's not to like? ∾ Lobster meat is available from your fishmonger – ask for uncooked tail meat. Alternatively, you could purchase a whole cooked lobster and break it apart to remove the meat, using a nutcracker to get all the meat from the legs. If you take this option you will need to reduce the cooking time so that the meat does not become overcooked and dry. ∾ *Serves 4*

30 ml olive oil

100 g butter

800 g rock lobster meat (preferably tail meat), cut into 2 cm dice

2 medium Roma tomatoes, diced

2 cloves garlic, chopped

1 chilli, seeded and chopped

10 basil leaves, finely chopped

100 ml dry vermouth

50 ml dry white wine

200 ml fish stock (see page 215)

sea salt and freshly ground black pepper

½ cup freshly chopped flat-leaf parsley

1 kg homemade fettuccine (see page 217)

Put a pot of salted water on to boil for the pasta. In a large, deep frying pan, heat the olive oil and 20 g of the butter. Seal the lobster until a little coloured. Add the tomato and cook for 2 minutes, then add the garlic, chilli and basil and fry until the garlic is golden. Pour in the vermouth and white wine and reduce the liquid by half. Add the stock and season to taste. Quickly stir in the remaining butter to melt it into the sauce. Throw in the parsley and turn the heat down to low.

Cook and drain the pasta, then toss it into the frying pan and mix through the sauce. Transfer to a large dish and take to the table to serve immediately.

VARIATION: For a more rustic version of this dish, purchase a whole live rock lobster, drown it in an ice slurry (your fishmonger can do this for you, if you prefer) and separate the legs from the body. Chop the lobster into sections using a sharp, heavy knife and cook it in the sections, leaving the shell on. You will have to work a little harder to get to the meat, but the flavour of the juices will be even more delicious.

Tortellini di patate e formaggio – Pasta filled with potato and Yarra Valley Persian fetta

Tortellini is by far my favourite filled pasta. When made with care, it has a crafted and elegant look – but the classic shape is not difficult to achieve once you have made it a few times. The variety of fillings and sauces is endless and only limited by your imagination. The filling described here requires waxy potatoes with a good flavour and excellent texture, so Spunta potatoes are ideal. Other varieties could be used, but avoid any that are too powdery. Persian fetta (see page 78) provides a great flavour, but if you prefer something more subtle, use fresh ricotta. ∾ *Serves 4*

1 kg homemade pasta dough (see page 217)

100 g butter

seeds and juice of 1 pomegranate

1 clove garlic, finely chopped

¼ cup freshly chopped sage

20 g freshly grated Parmigiano-Reggiano

¼ cup freshly chopped flat-leaf parsley

sea salt and freshly ground black pepper

POTATO AND FETTA FILLING

6 large waxy potatoes (preferably Spunta)

200 g Yarra Valley Persian fetta

200 g freshly grated Parmigiano-Reggiano

2 eggs

¼ cup finely chopped flat-leaf parsley

freshly ground black pepper

sea salt (optional)

To make the filling, boil the potatoes with their skins on until tender. Drain and allow to cool. Peel the potatoes and mash them until there are no lumps. Add the fetta, Parmigiano-Reggiano, eggs, parsley and a good pinch of pepper. You may need to add a bit of salt, but taste first as the fetta is already a little salty. Set the filling aside to cool and put a pot of water on to boil for the pasta.

On a floured surface, roll out the pasta dough into sheets (see page 217). Using an 8 cm round cutter (fluted, if you like), cut rounds until the dough is used up. Put the filling in a piping bag and pipe a small amount onto each round of dough. Brush a little cold water around the top edge, then fold the dough over to make a semi-circle. Take the two corners and bring them around to the middle, pressing together. You now have a tortellini. Continue until all the dough and filling have been used. Put the tortellini on a floured tray and set aside.

Melt the butter in a large pan and fry some of the pomegranate seeds with the garlic and sage. Cook the tortellini in the boiling water for 6–8 minutes so that they are still a little al dente, then drain and add to the frying pan. Stir in the remaining pomegranate seeds, pomegranate juice, Parmigiano-Reggiano and parsley and season to taste with salt and pepper. Serve immediately.

Torta di funghi e scalogno – Wild mushroom and shallot tart

The sweetness of the shallots is what makes this dish. You can use any variety of mushroom – there is a good selection available at all times of the year. The filling also makes a great side dish on its own. ➘ *Serves 4*

olive oil

100 g shallots, peeled but left whole

sea salt and freshly ground black pepper

250 ml chicken stock (see page 215)

100 g shiitake mushrooms

100 g enoki mushrooms

100 g oyster mushrooms

50 g Swiss brown mushrooms

100 g field mushrooms

100 g pine mushrooms

1 bay leaf

125 ml demi-glace (see page 216)

pinch of freshly chopped sage

leaves from 2 sprigs rosemary, chopped

4 × 10 cm shortcrust tart cases (see page 218), blind-baked

100 g frisée lettuce

extra-virgin olive oil

Preheat the oven to 180°C. Heat 150 ml olive oil in a frying pan and add the shallots. Sauté for 3–4 minutes until golden, stirring continuously so they do not burn. Season with salt and pepper and add the chicken stock. Cook over a low heat for 15 minutes or until tender.

Meanwhile, wash all the mushrooms and cut into bite-sized pieces. Heat 150 ml olive oil in a large pan and add the mushrooms and bay leaf. Cook until the thicker mushrooms are tender and the thinner ones are just soft. Add the demi-glace, sage and rosemary, season with salt and pepper and stir in the shallots.

Reheat the tart cases in the oven for a few minutes. Dress the frisée lettuce with extra-virgin olive oil. To serve, spoon some mushroom mixture and liquid into each tart case. Arrange some lettuce on the tarts and drizzle the plates with a little extra-virgin olive oil. Serve immediately.

Prosciutto con asparagi e nepitella – Prosciutto with asparagus, peas and catmint

Prosciutto is air-dried ham made from the hind leg of the pig. Traditionally, it is salted and left for about three weeks, then brushed clean and rubbed with *stuccatura* (a mixture of fat, salt and flour), then air-dried. (*Stuccatura* literally means 'plastering' and comes from the same etymological root as stucco.) The drying process should take at least nine months, although in some prosciutto-producing regions they specify fourteen months. With modern commercial dryers this time can be dramatically reduced and some prosciutto is released too early. Such a product will have an unpleasant soft, raw texture and be difficult to slice. ∿ In Italy the prosciutto of San Daniele is considered premium, and I always eat some when I am there. In Australia prosciutto is produced widely on a commercial scale, as well as by small artisanal producers. Don't be afraid to discuss curing times with your butcher or smallgoods manufacturer and have a hand in its production. Ask for prosciutto that is well seasoned, meaning that the meat is dry enough; too often we see it in the marketplace before it has been properly cured. Remember that prosciutto must always be sliced finely: thick slices can be overly chewy. ∿ I first came across catmint or *nepitella* (*Nepeta mussini*) in Tuscany, where it was being used to make pesto. Its leaves are smaller than other varieties of mint and the flavour is more delicate – ideal for spicing up savoury dishes such as in the dressing described here. The fresh, clean flavours of the catmint and asparagus balance the saltiness of the prosciutto perfectly. ∿ *Serves 4*

1 cup peas

200 g asparagus, trimmed and peeled

sea salt and freshly ground black pepper

500 g thinly sliced prosciutto

CATMINT DRESSING

1 cup catmint leaves

juice of 1 lemon

1 small clove garlic

2 tablespoons olive oil

sea salt and freshly ground black pepper

To make the dressing, wash the catmint in cold water and dry in a salad spinner or tea towel. Set a few leaves aside for the garnish and put the rest in a large mortar and pestle with the lemon juice, garlic, oil and a pinch of salt and pepper. Crush until there are no whole leaves left and the mixture is smooth.

Blanch the peas in boiling water, then refresh under cold water. Slice the asparagus spears thinly lengthways on a tight angle and combine with the peas, reserving a few peas for the garnish. Season with salt and pepper and add enough catmint dressing to coat all the vegetables.

To serve, lay a prosciutto slice on each plate, then spoon over some asparagus and peas. Continue layering until all the prosciutto and vegetables have been used. Sprinkle the reserved peas over and garnish with the reserved catmint leaves. Drizzle the remaining dressing over and serve.

Salmone arrosto con lenticchie – Roasted Atlantic salmon with lentils

With the reduced numbers of wild salmon in the world, farmed salmon has developed into a massive industry, and Australian farmed salmon has become very popular because of its consistent high quality. It is mainly produced in Tasmania and can be purchased in many forms, including cured or smoked. When selecting fresh salmon, make sure the flesh is firm with some spring to it. You must not overcook it or it will become very dry. The oily flesh and lovely texture of the fish go well with lentils and other pulses, and with mash. ∾ *Serves 4*

2 shallots, finely chopped

1 carrot, finely chopped

1 stalk celery, finely chopped

olive oil

300 ml red wine

100 ml port

100 ml sherry

sea salt and freshly ground black pepper

1 small onion, finely chopped

1 clove garlic, finely chopped

1 teaspoon pesto (see page 36)

250 g black lentils (preferably Casteluccio)

1 bay leaf

approximately 750 ml chicken stock
(see page 215)

4 × 200 g Atlantic salmon fillets

Fry half the shallot, carrot and celery in a small pot in a little olive oil until tender. Add the red wine, port and sherry. Reduce to a thick consistency and season with a little salt and pepper. Pass through a fine sieve or strainer and keep warm.

In a medium-sized pot, fry the onion, garlic and pesto in some olive oil with the remaining shallot, carrot and celery. Add the lentils and bay leaf and fry for 1 minute, then add half the stock. Season with a little salt and pepper and cook over a medium heat for about 30 minutes or until the stock has been absorbed and the lentils are tender but still holding their shape. If the lentils are not sufficiently cooked, add more stock and cook until it has been absorbed. Test again, repeating this process until the lentils are ready.

Preheat the oven to 200°C. Heat a little olive oil in an ovenproof frying pan and, when the oil is hot, add the salmon, flesh-side down. Season the skin-side with salt and pepper and cook for about 1 minute, then turn and cook the other side for 1 minute. Season the flesh side, then transfer the pan to the oven for 3 minutes. To serve, put a pile of lentils on each plate and top with a salmon fillet. Surround with the intense red-wine sauce and enjoy.

Pesce spada con olive e patate – Char-grilled swordfish with olives and potatoes

Swordfish is widely used in the kitchens of Sicilians. They have many ways of preparing this big-game fish, which is called 'the meat of the sea' because of its meaty texture. Most dishes using swordfish are very simple and require a quick cooking technique so that the fish does not become overcooked. Here, the potato and olive *ragù* provides a sharp backdrop of flavour to the fish. ～ *Serves 4*

olive oil

¼ cup freshly chopped flat-leaf parsley

sea salt and freshly ground black pepper

4 × 200 g swordfish fillets

extra-virgin olive oil

4 lemon wedges

POTATO AND OLIVE RAGÙ

2 teaspoons butter

1 clove garlic, finely chopped

1 teaspoon pesto (see page 36)

6 waxy potatoes (preferably Spunta), peeled and diced

2 Roma tomatoes, finely chopped

750 ml chicken stock (see page 215)

sea salt and freshly ground black pepper

handful of black olives, pitted

In a glass dish, mix 50 ml olive oil, a pinch of the parsley and some salt and pepper to taste. Add the swordfish and turn gently to cover thoroughly with the marinade. Refrigerate for 30 minutes.

Meanwhile, make the *ragù*. Melt the butter in a saucepan, add the garlic and pesto and sauté until the garlic takes on a little colour. Add the potato and fry a little, then add the tomato and 500 ml of the stock. Cook for 20 minutes over a medium heat until the stock has been absorbed. Season with a little salt and pepper and add the olives. Pour in the rest of the stock and continue cooking for 10 minutes until the potato is tender and the *ragù* is still quite moist. Preheat the char-grill to hot.

Put the swordfish on the hot char-grill and cook to medium-rare (about 2 minutes each side, depending on the thickness of the fillets). To serve, put a good spoonful of *ragù* in the centre of each plate and rest a swordfish fillet on it. Drizzle with some extra-virgin olive oil and garnish with a lemon wedge.

96

Calamari in padella con pomodoro al forno – Pan-fried calamari with oven-baked tomato

The terms 'calamari' and 'squid' are often used interchangeably. This can be very confusing, because 'calamari' refers to some, but not all, varieties of squid available in Australia, and cuttlefish (*seppie* in Italian) are also sometimes mistaken for calamari. The confusion is due to the fact that calamari, squid and cuttlefish (and octopus) are all cephalopods and similar in appearance. Squid and calamari are particularly alike and, in culinary terms, react in much the same way and can be interchanged successfully. The ink sacs can be removed and saved for making *ragù all'inchiostro* (for pasta or risotto), a slow-cooked dish. In contrast, the recipe that follows involves quick cooking. All of the calamari – body and tentacles – can be used. ∾ *Serves 4*

8 large Roma tomatoes, cored, halved and seeded

handful of parsley stalks

2 bay leaves

6 black peppercorns

sea salt and freshly ground black pepper

olive oil

800 g calamari, cleaned and cut into 3 cm pieces

100 g peas

2 cloves garlic, finely chopped

1 chilli, seeded and finely chopped

8 basil leaves, torn into shreds

juice of ½ lemon

¼ cup freshly chopped flat-leaf parsley

Preheat the oven to 120°C. Put the tomatoes in a small, deep baking tray with the parsley stalks, bay leaves and peppercorns. Season with salt and pepper and drizzle with olive oil. Roast for 1 hour until the oil starts to bubble and the tomatoes are tender. Remove from the oven and drain off the oil. Keep the tomatoes warm.

Lightly dust the calamari with flour and shake off the excess. Blanch the peas in boiling water for 5 minutes, then run under cold water. Heat 75 ml olive oil in a large frying pan and sauté the calamari quickly until golden. Add the peas, garlic, chilli and basil and cook until the garlic is golden. Season with salt and pepper and stir in the lemon juice and parsley.

To serve, arrange 4 tomato halves on each plate, top with calamari and drizzle olive oil around. Serve with a salad of soft green leaves, or perhaps radicchio.

La Famiglia

Any Italian will tell you they value their family above all. When you add a restaurant to the mix, the circle expands. What in other, non-Italian hands might be just a business becomes an extension of family life and culture, joined so seamlessly it is difficult to tell where one starts and the other finishes.

This is why the best Italian restaurants are family concerns, where family life and culture are totally integrated into dispensing hospitality. The tradition of the Florentino, reaching back to the Wynns, has always been about family, and this helps to explain the establishment's longevity. The resulting commitment, quality, service and warmth are beyond commercial measure and enhance every visit to a restaurant where the family is 'at home' to its guests.

Rinaldo Massoni devoted his life to the Florentino and then passed it to his son Leon, who recalls a childhood of playing in the kitchen, eating ice-cream in the cold larder and making pancakes. When George Tsindos took over, he ran it for many years with his son Raymond. 'I was taught that my commitment was to the business,' says Raymond. 'A good restaurant becomes your club, your footy team and your family – you can forget having those things outside.'

Guy Grossi would add that a restaurant is a child, just like any other child in a family. It is a living, breathing entity that needs daily nurturing to grow and develop, and will run wild if neglected. By the same token, the family doesn't exist without the business, so it demands sacrifice and a continual journey without arrival, on which you're joined by those staff who can push themselves and stay motivated. Obsessing about detail thus becomes a way of life.

Such is and was the ethos in and around the Florentino, where, as mentioned earlier, the immediate neighbourhood was dominated for decades by family-run Italian restaurants. As a community, they pioneered Melbourne's now-established food and restaurant culture, forging strong links within what was then a small Italian immigrant society. In addition, many of those involved had migrated together, worked together or run businesses together. They became affectionately known over time as Melbourne's 'Spaghetti Mafia'.

OPPOSITE, MAIN PICTURE
The Grossi era: Guy Grossi (standing, centre) with his family and staff. Seated, from left, are Guy's daughter, Loredana; his wife, Melissa; his son, Carlo; his mother and late father, Marisa and Pietro; his sister, Elizabeth; and Grossi Florentino's restaurant manager, Jeanette Barker. Standing behind Jeanette is Guy's brother-in-law and fellow chef, Chris Rodriguez.

Grossi Florentino continues as a family restaurant in every sense of the word. Guy's sister, Elizabeth, has perfected her front-of-house role since first working with Guy at Quadri restaurant in the 1980s. Her husband, chef Chris Rodriguez, is Guy's rock in the kitchen, without whom Guy says he could never have progressed so far, while Guy's wife, Melissa, works full-time administering the business.

Despite the Grossis' close involvement with the business during the week, they reserve Sundays purely for family. Their lively get-togethers ('feasts' by any other name) are attended by anyone and everyone – extended family, aged from eight months to eighty, and those who've grown close through the restaurant. Guy and his mother, Marisa, love to cook, while the late Pietro always enjoyed his *consigliere* advisory role. The linen, presentation, wine and flowers, whether the meal is served indoors or al fresco, are of a piece with Grossi Florentino and the whole event is marked by seductive, mouth-watering aromas and loud conversation.

'It's nice when you go to work because you have a sense of doing something that reflects your community,' says Guy. 'It's a very nice way to live.'

Cape sante al forno – Oven-baked scallops on the half-shell with an almond crust

Wild scallops from Spring Bay in Tasmania are the best Australian scallops I have found. They grow on the east coast of the island, 30–40 metres deep in some of the purest and coldest water in the world. The molluscs are a generous size and their flesh is firm. Here their sweetness is enhanced by the almonds and fresh herbs in the crust. ◠ *Serves 4*

100 g blanched almonds

4 teaspoons freshly chopped coriander

2 teaspoons freshly chopped dill

4 teaspoons freshly chopped flat-leaf parsley

1 clove garlic, finely chopped

1 chilli, seeded and finely chopped

grated zest of ½ lemon

100 g softened butter

16 scallops on the half-shell
(preferably Spring Bay)

100 g lamb's lettuce (mâche),
washed thoroughly

sea salt and freshly ground black pepper

extra-virgin olive oil

Preheat the oven to 200°C and toast the almonds until golden. Reduce the oven temperature to 180°C. Allow the nuts to cool, then chop finely.

Put the herbs, garlic and chilli in a large bowl. Mix in the chopped almonds and lemon zest. Add the butter and mix until the herbs, garlic and nuts are spread evenly through. Arrange the scallops on a baking sheet and spoon a little of the almond mixture onto each one. Bake for about 5 minutes or until the crusts are golden.

Put the lettuce in a bowl and season with salt and pepper. Drizzle lightly with olive oil and toss gently. To serve, put some salad in the centre of each plate and arrange 4 scallops around it.

Gamberi con porri, patate e finocchio – Prawns with leek-and-potato purée and fennel

Fresh prawns are easy to obtain these days, but the frozen product can be good too – as long as the original quality is high. Western Australian and South Australian prawns are great, but stay away from cheap imports from neighbouring countries, which are not as firm as local prawns and whose flavour is watery and bland. ⌒ *Serves 4–6*

1 large bulb fennel

white-wine vinegar

olive oil

½ cup finely chopped flat-leaf parsley

sea salt and freshly ground black pepper

2 cloves garlic, finely chopped

1 bay leaf

1 medium onion, chopped

2 large potatoes, peeled and chopped

1 leek, chopped

250–375 ml chicken stock (see page 215)

12–18 large prawns

pinch of freshly chopped chilli (optional)

To make the dressing (ingredients opposite), heat the vinegar and verjuice in a saucepan with the saffron and bay leaf. Reduce the liquid by half, then add the shallot and olive oil. Remove from the heat and season to taste. Whisk lightly and set aside to cool completely.

Using a sharp knife, shave 2 mm slices of fennel lengthways across the bulb. Put the slices in a bowl and dress with a little vinegar and olive oil. Sprinkle with a little of the parsley and season with salt and pepper. Toss lightly and set aside.

Fry half the garlic and the bay leaf in some olive oil in a medium-sized pot, then add the onion and sauté until golden. Add the potato and leek and cook until they have coloured a little, but not too much. Season with salt and pepper, add the chicken stock and cook over a medium heat for 20 minutes or until the potato is tender. Drain off and reserve any excess liquid (in case you need it to moisten the purée) and put the mixture in a food processor. Purée until thick and velvety smooth. Set aside and keep warm.

Peel the mid-section of the prawns and devein, leaving the head and tail intact (or remove the head, if you prefer). In a large pan, heat 20 ml olive oil.

106

SAFFRON DRESSING

125 ml white-wine vinegar

250 ml verjuice

10 saffron threads

1 bay leaf

3 shallots, finely diced

125 ml olive oil

sea salt and freshly ground black pepper

Add the prawns one at a time so as not to splash the oil and fry for 2 minutes on each side, or until golden. Add the remaining garlic, the chilli (if using) and a sprinkle of parsley. Season with salt and pepper and cook over a medium heat for 2–3 minutes.

To serve, spoon some leek-and-potato purée onto the centre of each plate, arrange 3 prawns on top and finish with some shaved fennel. Drizzle with saffron dressing.

Cacciucco alla livornese – Fish and tomato stew from Livorno

I once drove for nearly two hours from Chianti to get to Livorno, on the Tuscan coast, just so I could try the famous local dish *cacciucco* – and it was worth it. Traditionally, at least five varieties of fish and seafood are needed: one for each 'c' in the word *cacciucco*. It presents spectacularly in big bowls or on a serving dish and is one for licking your fingers after eating. ∾ *Serves 4–6*

olive oil

1 onion, chopped

2 cloves garlic, chopped

1 large carrot, chopped

2 stalks celery, chopped

1/4 cup freshly chopped sage

1/4 cup freshly chopped coriander

sea salt and freshly ground black pepper

4 tablespoons tomato paste

250 ml white wine

2 litres fish stock (see page 215)

4 red mullets, scaled and cleaned

8 prawns, shelled and deveined,
but with heads and tails intact

1 medium calamari tube, cut in half
lengthways and sliced across

8 mussels, cleaned and bearded

12 scallops, cleaned

1/2 cup finely chopped flat-leaf parsley

BRUSCHETTA

4–6 slices of stale casalinga bread

1 clove garlic, peeled

extra-virgin olive oil

Heat a little olive oil in a large pot. Sauté the onion, garlic, carrot, celery, sage and coriander until golden. Season to taste with salt and pepper. Add the tomato paste and cook until the paste has darkened a little, then add the white wine and reduce by half. Pour in the fish stock and simmer gently for 30 minutes.

Put a little more olive oil in a frying pan. Lightly sear the fish and shellfish in the order of time they will take to cook: the whole fish first, then the prawns, calamari, mussels and, finally, scallops. Sear each lightly on both sides and then add to the broth, stirring gently. Season with salt and pepper and simmer for 10 minutes or until the whole fish have cooked through.

Meanwhile, make the bruschetta by grilling the bread on both sides until golden brown. Rub with the garlic and drizzle with a little extra-virgin olive oil.

Ladle the *cacciucco* into large bowls and scatter with parsley. Serve with a slice of *bruschetta*.

Bistecca alla fiorentina – T-bone steak with sautéed green beans

This is one of the most famous – and simple – ways to cook steak in the entire Italian repertoire. The recipe comes from Tuscany, where the large, white cattle of the Val di Chiana are traditionally used. Whichever breed is used, the cut is always the same: the classic T-bone, incorporating the fillet and loin of the beast. Quality is everything with this dish. For years I've used low-line Black Angus ox, which has been bred back to its origins. The meat is marbled and flavoursome and the size works very well for this particular cut. ∿ Because they come from such large cattle, these steaks are usually ordered for two people. On one occasion, in a trattoria in Chianti, my son and I ordered one to share and although neither of us is a shy eater, the steak got the better of us! *Bistecca alla fiorentina* is traditionally served with green beans. ∿ *Serves 4*

300 g green beans, topped and tailed

4 × 250 g T-bone steaks

sea salt and freshly ground black pepper

leaves from 1 sprig rosemary, chopped

2 teaspoons butter

1 clove garlic, finely chopped

extra-virgin olive oil

4 large lemon wedges

Preheat the char-grill to hot. Blanch the beans in a saucepan of boiling, salted water for 5 minutes (or longer, if you prefer them to be more tender), then drain and refresh in cold water. Lay the steaks on the grill and seal well before turning them – they should have dark grill lines seared into the flesh. Season with salt and pepper and sprinkle with rosemary. (Never put salt on beef that has yet to be sealed – it extracts moisture, making the meat dry.) Cook the steaks until they are just under your desired likeness, then leave them to rest and keep warm.

In a large pan, melt the butter and add the garlic. Cook until the butter has turned slightly golden. Add the green beans and toss until hot. Brush the steaks with a little olive oil and return to the char-grill to finish cooking. To serve, arrange some beans on each plate and lay a steak next to them. Garnish with a generous wedge of lemon and finish with a drizzle of extra-virgin olive oil.

Vitello ai funghi – Veal with mushroom ragù

This dish has appeared on our menus many times over the years and remains as popular as ever. Great-quality veal that has been properly trimmed is important here – talk to your butcher about the meat available through the year. Use your favourite variety of mushroom and serve with roasted potatoes or roesti. ～ *Serves 4–6*

1 × 1.5 kg veal topside, cut into 5 mm slices

50 g butter

300 g Swiss brown *or* button mushrooms, sliced

pinch of freshly chopped sage

125 ml white wine

30 ml cream

sea salt and freshly ground black pepper

60 ml demi-glace (optional; see page 216)

MUSHROOM RAGÙ

100 g mixed dried wild mushrooms

500 ml water

1 onion, finely sliced

1 clove garlic, chopped

2 teaspoons olive oil

1 bay leaf

1 tablespoon tomato paste

250 ml red wine

To make the *ragù*, soak the dried mushrooms in the water for at least 1 hour, or overnight if possible. Lift the mushrooms from their soaking water and drain well, reserving the liquid. Chop the mushrooms. In a large pot, sauté the onion and garlic in the olive oil. Stir in the mushrooms and bay leaf, then add the tomato paste and stir until it has caramelised. Add the red wine and reduce by half. Add the reserved mushroom liquid and reduce again over a medium heat until the mixture is thick and rich.

Bash the veal slices with a mallet to tenderise them. Dust with flour and shake off the excess. Melt the butter in a large frying pan and seal the meat, then add the fresh mushrooms and sage. When the mushrooms have taken on a little colour, deglaze the pan with the white wine. Transfer the veal to a warm dish. Stir the mushroom *ragù* and cream into the pan and cook for a few minutes until well incorporated. Season lightly with salt and pepper to taste. Add the demi-glace, if using, then return the veal to the pot and allow it to heat through for 1–2 minutes. Serve immediately.

Coniglio in porchetta – Rabbit filled with pork stuffing

The word *porchetta* traditionally refers to pork cooked with herbs and spices, but here it applies to rabbit prepared in the spirit of the original dish. Rabbit with pig flavours sounds odd, but you won't think so once you've tried it. I use farmed rabbits because they are raised in controlled conditions and if you buy farmed rabbits, you know you will be getting tender, young meat rather than old, tough specimens. ∾ *Serves 6*

1 × 1 kg rabbit

300 g speck, sliced into thin strips

1 onion, roughly chopped

1 carrot, roughly chopped

1 stalk celery, roughly chopped

sea salt and freshly ground black pepper

3–4 sprigs rosemary

approximately 2 litres chicken stock

(see page 215)

PORK STUFFING

600 g pork mince

2 cloves garlic, finely chopped

2 teaspoons pesto (see page 36)

¼ cup freshly chopped sage

¼ cup freshly chopped rosemary leaves

1 chilli, seeded and finely chopped

½ teaspoon fennel seeds

1 egg

sea salt and freshly ground black pepper

Preheat the oven to 180°C. Lay the rabbit on your work surface so that the belly is facing you. Using a boning knife and starting on one side of the rib cage, make a cut near the point of the ribs and follow the bones down with the knife, cutting between the bones and the meat so that you are separating them and the meat is left in a large sheet. Continue all the way down to the spine, making sure not to cut any holes in the meat. Do this to the other side until you reach the spine, then gently cut along the length, still making sure not to puncture the meat. You should be left with one large piece. (If you prefer, ask your butcher to bone the rabbit, leaving the meat in one large piece.) Discard the bones and put the meat to one side while you make the stuffing.

To make the stuffing, put the pork, garlic, pesto, herbs, spices and egg in a large bowl. Season with salt and pepper and mix thoroughly. Lay the rabbit on your work surface and spoon the stuffing down the centre in a long log. Roll up tightly and lay the strips of speck over and around to cover the whole piece. Truss the rabbit with kitchen string so that it will keep its shape.

Scatter the onion, carrot and celery in a baking tray and sit the stuffed rabbit on top. Sprinkle with a little salt and pepper, add the rosemary sprigs and pour enough stock into the tray to cover the vegetables. Bake for about 45 minutes, basting from time to time. If the tray dries out, add a little more stock.

Transfer the meat to a warm dish and cover. Reduce the pan juices to a light jus, then strain into a jug. Serve the meat and glazed vegetables drizzled with jus.

NOTE: For even tastier juices, add a little wine to the roasting tray after you have removed the meat and vegetables. Simmer for a few minutes, strain and serve.

Guancia – Ox cheek braised in red wine

Ox cheek is a gelatinous meat cut that has many applications. Added to a *bollito misto* (mixed boiled meats) it will make the soup rich with flavour, while cold boiled cheek is fantastic in a salad served with *salsa verde*. You can obtain ox cheeks from a good butcher, but you may need to order them in advance. ❧ *Serves 4*

4 ox cheeks

olive oil

3 medium onions, chopped

1 clove garlic, chopped

1 large carrot, chopped

2 stalks celery, chopped

1 teaspoon ground juniper berries

1 teaspoon ground star anise

¼ cup freshly chopped sage

1 bay leaf

3 tablespoons tomato paste

1 litre red wine

sea salt and freshly ground black pepper

CELERIAC PURÉE

2 medium celeriac

1 litre milk

sea salt and freshly ground black pepper

handful of freshly grated Parmigiano-Reggiano

Preheat the oven to 180ºC. Trim any excess sinew and gristle from the ox cheeks. In a hot pan with a little olive oil, seal the meat until dark in colour. In a large pot, fry the onion, garlic, carrot, celery, spices and herbs until very rich in colour. Add the tomato paste and cook for about 5 minutes, ensuring it doesn't burn. Pour in the red wine and add the ox cheeks. Cover with water and season with a little salt and pepper. Transfer carefully to a baking tray and cover with foil. Bake for 1–1½ hours or until the meat is tender.

Meanwhile, make the celeriac purée. Peel the bitter skin off the celeriac and chop the flesh into small pieces. Put in a pot, cover with the milk, season with a little salt and pepper and cook over a medium heat for 20 minutes or until tender. Drain. Purée in a food processor and return to the pot. Add the Parmigiano-Reggiano, adjust the seasoning and keep warm.

Transfer the ox cheeks to a warm dish and rest in a warm place for a few minutes. With the back of a ladle, push the braising juices firmly through a fine strainer into a saucepan. Return the meat to the sauce and warm gently on the stove. To serve, spoon some celeriac purée onto the centre of each plate. Put an ox cheek on top and spoon the sauce over and around. Serve immediately.

Mille foglie – Pastry layers of summer berries and mascarpone cream

This dessert of berries and pastry layered with cream, similar to the French *millefeuille* (meaning 'a thousand layers'), can be made with a variety of ingredients. For a different effect, try substituting *crostoli* or a biscuit for the puff pastry. ∾ *Serves 4–6*

1 × 30 cm × 30 cm sheet of puff pastry (see page 218)

150 g blueberries

150 g blackberries

caster sugar

1 tablespoon powdered gelatine

150 g raspberries

150 g redcurrants

450 ml cream

grated zest of ½ lemon

350 g mascarpone cheese

50 g flaked almonds, toasted

icing sugar

Preheat the oven to 200°C. Lay the pastry on a tray and prick well with a fork. Bake for 10–12 minutes or until golden. Cool. Cook the blueberries, blackberries and 100 g caster sugar in a pot over a medium heat for 4–5 minutes, or until liquid comes out of the berries but they remain whole. Take care not to burn them. Dissolve the gelatine in a little boiling water and add to the pot, then stir in the raspberries and redcurrants. Transfer to a bowl and chill until firm.

Whip the cream, lemon zest and a further 80 g caster sugar until stiff peaks form. In a separate bowl, whip the mascarpone cheese for 1–2 minutes until it firms a little, then gently fold it into the cream. Cut the pastry sheet into 3 even pieces. On one piece of pastry, spread some of the cream mixture to a thickness of about 2 cm, then spread evenly with half the cold berry mixture. Put another length of pastry on top and repeat, reserving some of the cream. Put the remaining pastry sheet on top and gently press down. Using a palette knife, smooth the reserved cream over the sides and ends of the log. Carefully press the toasted almonds onto the cream and dust the top lightly with icing sugar. Refrigerate for at least 2 hours before serving.

To serve, slice carefully with a sharp, serrated knife, using a sawing motion. Stand the slices up on serving plates and accompany with berry coulis, if desired.

Semifreddo croccante – Praline semifreddo

The term *croccante* ('crisp') is used to describe desserts that include crunchy praline, while *semifreddo* means 'half-frozen' – the mixture is put in the freezer, but because of its sugar level it does not freeze fully. It's a great way of making a frozen dessert without having to use an ice-cream machine. The recipe given here is extremely versatile and can be adapted to many other flavours. It makes a very large amount, but works best in these quantities and keeps well in the freezer. Make it the next time you're having a party! ∾ *Serves 24*

80 g caster sugar

80 g liquid glucose

200 g honey

5–6 egg whites (total of 150 ml)

900 ml cream, lightly whipped

PRALINE

100 g toasted almonds

100 g caster sugar

To make the praline, scatter the almonds on a lightly greased baking sheet. Heat the sugar with a splash of water in a saucepan over medium heat, stirring gently so it doesn't burn. When the mixture is light brown, pour it over the almonds and allow to cool. Wrap in a clean tea towel and crush very finely with a mallet or heavy object.

Put the sugar, glucose and honey in a saucepan and heat for 4–6 minutes until the mixture bubbles and thickens slightly, but does not change colour (if you have a cooking thermometer, the temperature should reach 125°C – but remember to stir the ingredients before you measure the temperature, so an accurate reading can be taken). Remove from the heat and allow to cool for 5 minutes (to just above 90°C). Meanwhile, start whipping the egg whites. When the honey mixture has cooled for 5 minutes (or reaches 90°C), begin pouring it slowly into the egg whites, mixing gently until well combined. Allow to cool in the bowl for 5 minutes, then fold in the cream and praline. Pour into two 40 cm × 7 cm × 7 cm plastic- or silicon-lined terrine moulds and freeze. To turn out, dip a knife in hot water and run it around the edges of the mould. Slice and serve with fresh berries or fruit purée, if desired.

NOTE: The semifreddo can be poured into individual moulds (5 cm deep), if preferred. Turn out to serve.

Zuppa inglese – Trifle of sponge cake, berries and pastry cream

The origins of this curiously named 'English soup' are very obscure. There are as many versions as there are cookbooks, but they all use pastry cream and sponge cake. The name probably refers to the custard, or *crème anglaise*, used in the trifle, which is layered with the cake in a manner reminiscent of other traditional Italian dishes such as lasagne. *Zuppa inglese* is served in many restaurants in Italy, especially in more casual establishments. Some versions are decorated with peaks of meringue lightly coloured with a blowtorch. ❧ Alchermes is a very aromatic, crimson-coloured liqueur with a long history in Italian cooking. It is made with spices and flavoured with rose and jasmine. You can substitute another liqueur (such as *cassis*) to suit your taste, if you prefer. ❧ *Serves 8–10*

100 g blueberries

100 g blackberries

60 g caster sugar

1–1½ tablespoons powdered gelatine

100 g boysenberries

100 g raspberries

500 ml cream, whipped

500 ml pastry cream (see page 219)

100 ml Alchermes liqueur

150 ml sugar syrup (see page 218)

extra fresh berries

icing sugar

To make the sponge cake (ingredients opposite), preheat the oven to 180°C. Grease a 20 cm springform tin well with the butter and line the bottom of the tin with baking paper. Put the eggs, egg yolks, sugar, honey and lemon zest in a double boiler and whisk until warm but not hot (if you have a cooking thermometer, the temperature should be 40°C). Meanwhile, sift the flour and baking powder together. Remove the honey mixture from the heat and, using an electric mixer, whip until nearly tripled in volume. Gently sift the flour and baking powder over and, using a wooden spoon, fold until there are no lumps. Pour the batter into the tin and bake for 30–40 minutes or until a skewer comes out clean. Cool in the tin for about 5 minutes, then remove to a wire rack and carefully peel the paper off. Allow to cool completely.

SPONGE CAKE

2 teaspoons butter

3 eggs

3 egg yolks

150 g caster sugar

1–1½ tablespoons honey

1 teaspoon grated lemon zest

100 g flour

¼ teaspoon baking powder

Put the blueberries, blackberries and caster sugar in a pot and cook over a medium heat for 4–5 minutes, or until the sugar dissolves and liquid comes out of the berries but they remain whole. Take care not to burn the berries. Dissolve the gelatine in a little boiling water and add to the berries, stirring. Add the boysenberries and raspberries and mix gently. Transfer to a bowl and refrigerate until the mixture starts to firm but is still pliable.

Gently fold half the cream into the pastry cream and blend well. Fold in the remaining cream. In a separate wide bowl, mix the liqueur and sugar syrup. Cut the sponge cake into 1 cm slices.

To construct the finished dish, take a large (2 litre) serving bowl. Lightly soak some cake slices in the liqueur, then put them in the serving bowl in a single layer. Spread with cream and berries. Repeat, gently pressing the layers together after each addition, and making sure you reserve 1 cup of the jelly from the berries. When you reach the rim of the bowl, soak the last slices of cake in liqueur and press them on top. Barely melt the reserved jelly over a low heat and brush liberally over the top of the cake. Decorate with fresh berries and dust with icing sugar. Refrigerate for at least 2 hours before serving (or overnight, if possible).

VARIATION: For a more elegant dessert, make the *zuppa inglese* in small individual moulds, as shown here. Turn out onto serving plates and garnish with a small purée of berries.

Panforte

Panforte, the spiced, flat cake of Siena, dates from medieval times. It is considered quite a treat and is eaten all year round after lunch or dinner, or as an afternoon nibble with coffee. Its spicy richness suggests a Middle Eastern heritage. The widely produced commercial varieties are generally of high quality, but it is very rewarding to make your own. ⌒ *Makes approximately 100 small pieces*

250 g nuts (a mixture of almonds, hazelnuts, pecans and walnuts)

150 g honey

60 g caster sugar

60 g dark chocolate (preferably Valrhona)

120 g dried fruit (a mixture of figs, apricots, pears, dates and cherries)

75 g flour

2 tablespoons cocoa

1 teaspoon cinnamon

6–8 × 15 cm × 2.5 cm sheets rice paper

icing sugar

Preheat the oven to 170°C. Toast the nuts until golden. Remove the skins from the hazelnuts by rubbing the nuts in a damp cloth.

Put the honey, sugar and chocolate in a medium-sized saucepan over a medium heat until the chocolate has melted and the sugar has dissolved. Meanwhile, combine the nuts, dried fruit, flour, cocoa and cinnamon in a large mixing bowl. Add the honey mixture and, using a wooden spoon, mix until a large, glossy ball has formed.

Grease your work surface, then gently roll out small amounts of the batter into logs 4 cm wide and running the length of the rice paper. Roll up in the rice paper and wrap each log in foil. Put the logs on a baking tray and bake for 12–15 minutes. Allow to cool in the foil.

Remove the foil and slice the panforte into 5 mm rounds, or thicker if you prefer. Dust with icing sugar to serve. The panforte will keep for weeks in an airtight container.

The Restaurant

The Restaurant is Grossi Florentino's gastronomical and architectural heart. Stepping up the curved staircase from the foyer to the two opulent rooms on the first floor is to be embraced by old-world Italian hospitality as it has been practised six days a week for over seventy-five years.

It is to participate in Rinaldo Massoni's dream, kept alive by several owners, of combining good food, wine and company in visually splendid surroundings. Turn left at the top of the stairs and you enter the inner Mural Room (tables 17 to 38), so named for its nine famous murals inspired by Renaissance Florentine and Tuscan life. Turn right and you are in the Wynn Room (tables 1 to 15), the original Cafe Florentino and former Cafe Denat, now named for Samuel Wynn.

Cafe Florentino was less grand and expensive than the French-style Cafe Denat it replaced, and it thrived so well under Massoni's hospitable management that he decided to expand. Tuscans have a flair for combining art and commerce and Rinaldo's vision was ahead of its time and very bold in the midst of the Great Depression. He bought the adjoining building, occupied by Edments jewellery store, and knocked a hole in the wall. He then spared no expense in creating a dining experience that would stimulate all the senses, employing as his architect the up-and-coming Roy Grounds, who was already a Cafe Florentino regular.

When it opened in 1934, the new 'inside' room was the epitome of contemporary chic, with a magnificent parquetry floor, ornately decorated ceiling, timber wall panelling (allegedly made from railway packing cases), wrought-iron wall lamps crafted by Emilio Gavotto, leather-upholstered chairs, and telephones on every table. 'The defining feature was the murals painted by students of Napier Waller (see pages 140–3).

129

Social columnist 'Annette' gushed thus about the opening of the new room on 5 August:

When I tell a tale of one long table seating 60 smart diners, smoking between courses, Continental fashion, eating by candlelight, chatting in English, Italian and French, with a background of frescoes showing glimpses of mediaeval Florentine life – then some will say, 'Ah, yes, perhaps . . . but not in Melbourne!' And out of my wisdom, I reply firmly, 'In Melbourne and last night . . .' For at a long table in a rollicking European atmosphere 60 men and women, including a representative from Government House, the Lord Mayor and his young wife, an eminent and knightly politician, an Admiral, an actress the world worships, and many attractive girls, gathered as the guests of Signor and Signora Massoni, who have brought their surroundings in Florence to Melbourne, and who showed the finished result at this particular party.

The new room, whose splendour was an excuse for more elaborate service and higher prices, continued to outshine the old Wynn Room even when Roy Grounds extensively refurbished the latter after a 1935 electrical fire. Being Melbourne, this predilection for the new over the old related entirely to the age of one's money. Human nature being what it is, the inside room assumed an allure over the outside room that prevails in some quarters even now, when the prices and the experience are equal. Philip Jones, writer and protégé of art patrons John and Sunday Reed, recalls that the Reeds and their kind thought the new room a little 'outré'. Sunday, born a Baillieu, dined at Cafe Florentino when it opened in the year of her marriage to John, and never sat anywhere other than in the 'old room'. Similarly, R.G. Casey (later Lord Casey and Governor-General of Australia) and his wife, Maie, preferred the far left corner of the outside room, and a table was always kept for them there.

One of the first **regular luncheon groups** to settle in was the Foreign Legion Club of prominent businessmen and professionals. They lunched on Fridays, occupying an oblong table where the staircase is now, from which they plotted practical jokes on the host they nicknamed 'Ginger'. These developed a different tone after Rinaldo checkmated them over some 1927 florins they persuaded him to buy for 25 pence each, recalls Leon. When Rinaldo found out, he charged them 25 pence for splits of mineral water correctly priced at tenpence.

ABOVE **Rinaldo Massoni, seated
at right, beside Bruno
Commonello-Smith, the
Florentino's manager and leader
of the local Fascist Party.
Behind them (centre) is George
Tsindos, then a young waiter.**

An immensely charming, tactful and greatly liked host, Rinaldo was also a meticulous restaurateur. As the business prospered despite the Depression, he moved his family from Carlton to Brighton, whence he would arrive every day at 11.30 a.m., having parked his car at Lane's Motors around the corner in Exhibition Street. His nephew Mario Virgona worked in the wine shop and could see him coming. Leon recalls, 'If he looked like he'd had a night on the turps or had lost at the races and was in a bad mood, Mario would rattle his keys on the brass handrail as Dad went up the stairs. Once there, bad mood or not, he'd have the whole dining room reset if he glimpsed even a speck of dust on a table.'

In 1939 Rinaldo decided to revisit Italy with his daughter Lolita, whom he hoped to dissuade from marrying the head waiter, Ivan Kuketz (which she did anyway). It was 'His First Holiday', as headlined in the *Argus*:

. . . it is rare to find the customer entertaining the seller and yet about 60 men, including a sprinkling of knights, medicos and leaders in industry, joined together the other evening to express good wishes to a man whose patrons they have been during the past years. The person they honoured was Rinaldo Massoni, whose restaurant, named after his native town, is now known all over the world.

Rinaldo and Lolita had got no further than Ceylon, however, when **World War II broke out.** Back in Melbourne, this posed enormous problems for Cafe Florentino when Italy joined Hitler in March 1940. The authorities rounded up all the Italian members of what George Tsindos said was a harmless local Fascist group. Their leader, unfortunately, was the Florentino's manager, Bruno Commonello-Smith. He, his brother and several other key staff disappeared that very day into an internment camp (which, Commonello-Smith later told George, was six years of holidays where they had more food than they could eat and every possible appliance to cook it with).

At Cafe Florentino, Rinaldo was in tears. Not all his employees had been taken, but they joined the customers in choosing to stay away. George rang the staff and persuaded them to come in, a favour Rinaldo never forgot. Business was so bad, however, that Rinaldo nearly closed the restaurant and even offered it to the Red Cross as a rest-and-recreation refuge in 1941. Then he died suddenly of a heart attack, aged only forty-nine, followed six weeks later by his wife, Grace. Leon was sixteen and too young to take over, so his father's trustees appointed as manager Jock McPherson, a former police superintendent. Leon, until then a pampered only son dressed in handmade suits and the centre of an adoring Italian world, found himself living with Uncle Jimmy Watson and family – still immersed in food, wine and hospitality, but a decidedly Aussie version. Despite being half-Italian himself, Jimmy had no time for Italians.

While Leon languished, his inheritance flourished. In 1942, Americans serving in the Pacific began pouring into Melbourne on leave and headed straight for Cafe Florentino. Great lovers of Italian food, they would queue to the corner of Exhibition Street waiting for the restaurant to open at 6 p.m. Thus both Australia and the Florentino were saved by the Americans.

This was the business Leon joined in 1946 when, at twenty-one, he stepped in as Victoria's youngest-ever licensee – a pretty naive fellow, he says, over whom the waiters and chefs had the upper hand. Wartime price controls remained in place and no dish could cost more than five shillings (50 cents). Accordingly, grilled whiting was the equivalent of 36 cents, lamb cutlets were 30 cents and lemon pancakes 10 cents.

'My formal training was minimal and I was constantly reminded by the oldies who were trying it on of what Dad did, like give them beer or whisky, neither of which was permitted under the licence. In the kitchen we had an *abayeur*, or barker, who called every order,' says Leon. 'There were no culinary controls and you had to check all the dockets, which was a very big job. Meanwhile, the back door was kept locked, otherwise supplies came in the front and went straight out again.

'People wonder why I'm a tough old bugger. They were all great fellows, but you couldn't trust them as far as you could throw them. During the war the restaurants were a haven for illegal immigrants and escaped prisoners of war, but we asked no questions if they could do the job. The military police would come around and the then Minister of Immigration, Arthur Calwell, would have been waited on by an illegal the night before. We knew and he did too and he helped a lot of them. But the police blitzes were such that one day you'd have staff and the next you'd have none.'

OPPOSITE **A portrait of Rinaldo Massoni, given by his son, Leon, whose restaurants it adorned over the years, now watches over the Wynn Room. Artist Mirka Mora cleaned the portrait in 1999. Behind are jars of fruit bottled by the Grossi family.**

After the war it was a different scene. Many refugees and so-called enemy aliens (Europeans deported and interned during the war) turned out to be highly trained professionals from world-class hotels such as London's Dorchester and Savoy, and so began **an era of marvellous food and service** from which all the restaurants and hotel dining rooms benefited.

'Those early days standing at the head of the stairs and fronting up in the dining room were no mean feat,' Leon recalls. 'It reached the stage where it got to me and I wanted to get out. I'd always been fond of George Tsindos, who had Monte Vista, a guesthouse at Sorrento. He'd waited at the Florentino in the thirties and knew the background, so we went fifty-fifty and he came in to help run it.' George said he couldn't raise a bank loan to buy Leon out, so he borrowed against his life insurance policy to buy in. So began, in September 1950, their successful thirteen-year partnership. George sorted out the kitchen, which he allegedly found was going through an impossibly high number of chickens each day. 'When I told the poultry man I wanted only one case, I found he didn't have another two to take away,' said George. 'The fishmonger came in at the same time and I said, "I hope you're not doing that." A whole side of bacon disappeared and the French chef got embarrassed and left when I pointed it out.'

John and Sunday Reed always dined (never lunched) at the Restaurant when in town, and Philip Jones recalls his first visits with them in the 1950s. It was a treat, he says, to indulge in the then uncommon delicacy of avocado served with three dipping sauces, pink roast lamb encrusted with nuts, and chocolate soufflé. He recalls one hot summer evening in the late 1950s dining with the Reeds and artists Joy Hester and Grey Smith (the painter for whom Hester left her husband, Albert Tucker): 'We were at a table by the open window, and wafting in were the sounds of waltzes and foxtrots from the dance school opposite. Joy grabbed Grey's arm, saying, "Come on, we're going to join them", and we saw them dodging trams across Bourke Street. Next thing they were whirling about and waving from the window.'

The Reeds always dined with **artists and intellectuals**, many of whom went on to become household names under their patronage. When painter and writer Mirka Mora and her husband, Georges, first dined at Cafe Florentino in 1952 it was

134

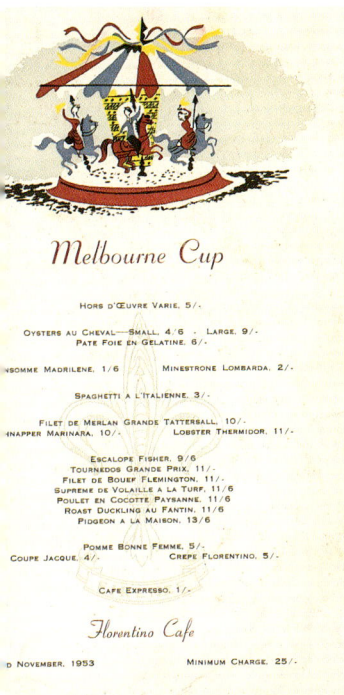

Melbourne Cup

HORS D'ŒUVRE VARIE. 5/-

OYSTERS AU CHEVAL—SMALL. 4/6 . LARGE. 9/-
PATE FOIE EN GELATINE. 6/-

ʃSOMME MADRILENE. 1/6   MINESTRONE LOMBARDA. 2/-

SPAGHETTI A L'ITALIENNE. 3/-

FILET DE MERLAN GRANDE TATTERSALL. 10/-
NNAPPER MARINARA. 10/-   LOBSTER THERMIDOR. 11/-

ESCALOPE FISHER. 9/6
TOURNEDOS GRANDE PRIX. 11/-
FILET DE BOUEF FLEMINGTON. 11/-
SUPREME DE VOLAILLE A LA TURF. 11/6
POULET EN COCOTTE PAYSANNE. 11/6
ROAST DUCKLING AU FANTIN. 11/6
PIDGEON A LA MAISON. 13/6

POMME BONNE FEMME. 5/-
COUPE JACQUE. 4/-   CREPE FLORENTINO. 5/-

CAFE EXPRESSO. 1/-

Florentino Cafe

D NOVEMBER. 1953   MINIMUM CHARGE. 25/-

ABOVE **The Melbourne Cup carnival has long been celebrated at the Florentino with special menus, such as this one from 1953.**

with the Reeds, Arthur Boyd, Hester and Smith. 'It was our first big outing together and then we went very often,' says Mirka. 'It was the only decent place at the time and we lived at 9 Collins Street, so it was just a hop, a skip and a jump for lunch or dinner.' Her sons, William, Philippe and Tiriel, are now Cellar Bar habitués.

Mirka, who says she lives above her means, still frequents the Restaurant, observed by Rinaldo's portrait, which she cleaned some years ago with saliva on cotton wool (the best method, she claims), revealing a ring on his left hand. 'I often go by myself to reminisce and think of all the people who are no more. We went a lot with John and Sunday in the fifties.' Mirka, French by birth, claims the food was 'not so good', but she went for the atmosphere and the quality of the people. 'All the intelligentsia, big businessmen, writers and wealthy painters were there. The staff knew who you were when you arrived, which is the secret of a good restaurant. It should be welcoming in the grand manner. Then, as now, the Florentino was grand in the theatrical tradition and mostly a sort of celebration. You always knew you'd meet interesting people from elsewhere and interstate.'

People had fun despite the stringent licensing laws and because of the Italians' predilection for flouting inconvenient regulations. Designed to allow food and drink between 6 and 8 p.m. only, after which all liquor was supposed to be off the table, the laws were an excuse for much creative circumvention. Since the only exception to the 6–8 p.m. rule was an extension until 10 p.m. for birthdays and 'special parties', every Monday saw a line of restaurateurs at the Liquor Commission armed with requests for six days of birthday celebrations. Cafe Florentino also operated under an Australian Wine Licence, which disallowed spirits and beer, *and* it was a tied house, since under the terms of the lease with Sammy Wynn, the Florentino could serve only his wines.

Only those known to the house were served alcohol other than wine: waiters would check and be given a pink slip by Leon. 'We always had spirits and if there was a raid anything resembling alcohol was served in coffee cups,' he says. 'The Triacas and I had boxes made for the spirits and liqueurs. They kept theirs under a false step at the Latin, and the Florentino had a secret staircase. It was all very speakeasy but seemed quite normal to us.' When one restaurant was raided, its staff would ring around and warn the others. 'Then there was the problem of the Wynns coming in and seeing that we were serving not just their wines, which were pretty ordinary at the time. Despite the tie, I decided "Bugger it" and served anything. During the war we were allowed to because of the shortage, and afterwards I wasn't going back. I think Sammy knew, but they were a wonderful family and didn't make an issue of it.'

Restaurateurs nurtured patrons to ensure repeat business among the few thousand people who ate out regularly. Every night Leon would know who was coming and at what time, what they would eat and when they would leave. 'If I put my prices up by sixpence they'd go up the road to Molina's, then Joe would put his up and they'd come back to me. We'd laugh about it over a beer and say, "Who'd you get this week?" Friday and Saturday nights were always booked out with regulars and I still remember where they sat. We might have two people at a table for four and match them up with a couple who hadn't booked. It's unthinkable now to ask people to share a table and it was quite an art. But it led to some wonderful friendships and created a genuine cafe society.'

Melbourne was a sophisticated town in the early 1960s, says Peter Rowland. There was a group who skied in Europe every year, holidayed at Portsea and was the Mural Room's core clientele, he says, **Melbourne's 'triple A social list'.** The group included names such as the Napthines, Laycocks, Matears, Joan and Noel Dixon, Nathans and Clemengers. Rowland was a keen surfer at the time, renting a fibro shack at the rear of Monte Vista, the Tsindos guesthouse at Sorrento. Every weekend George and his wife, Mabel, ran a restaurant on the guesthouse balcony for the Portsea jet set, where they served lasagne from the Florentino and cooked steaks, with Rowland helping out on Saturday nights – the best-kept secret on the Peninsula, he says.

When Rowland started his catering business, he, too, got *lasagne verdi* from the Florentino, the only place in town that made it. This cosy arrangement ended, however, with a misunderstanding over the shack that resulted in George banning Rowland from the Florentino. He kept going, however, because the staff would ring to tell him when George wasn't there, and he continued buying the lasagne under an assumed name. Eventually he was sprung and forced to exit through the kitchen with George in pursuit.

This was an invigorating period that saw Wynn's old wine bar transformed into Il Bistro, followed by the opening of the Bistro Grill. The business effectively

BELOW **Peter Rowland, faithful customer and one-time manager of the Florentino.**

doubled during the 1950s, with all the pressures that entailed, not least on Leon's marriage. Once again he'd had enough and, intent on pursuing a career as a wine merchant, he sold his share to George in 1963 without regrets.

George's involvement continued for another seventeen years, based on the philosophy that you don't change a winning recipe. Eighteen staff took long-service leave during his tenure and indeed it was said that under George (and, later, Branco Tocigl) someone had to die for a waiter to secure a Florentino job.

And so the Florentino acquired the atmosphere of a club, of a home away from home (albeit a rather grand one) where regulars felt relaxed, comfortable and feted. The food was always fresh and beautifully presented, the atmosphere grand but not overwhelming, and the diners grew accustomed to a system of food and friendliness about which they were educated over generations.

In the two decades following World War II, all the Italian restaurants were patronised by the same people, most of whom knew each other and wanted their regular tables and waiters. Sir Rupert and Lady (Kath) Clarke; the Caseys; Sir Dallas Brooks, Victoria's Governor; prime ministers Robert Menzies, Harold Holt and William McMahon; Country Party leader Jack McEwen; and Opposition leaders past (Dr Evatt) and present (Arthur Calwell) were Florentino regulars, as was Malcolm Fraser, who began coming with his father, Neville, when he was a teenager. Adding to the mix were others prominent in their day, including chic Melbourne businesswoman Frances Burke, a Florentino fixture for about thirty years, whose heyday was from the early 1950s to the late '60s. 'All feathers and pearls and a cheeky hat, she would come to the top of the stairs, swivel her eyes and ask for a well-placed table,' says Philip Jones. 'If she was dining with the Caseys, she'd do a gracious table-hop before she reached them. That was how business was done in a decorous manner. She was Melbourne's respectable lesbian, though she pretended otherwise, and her friendship with the Caseys gave her a certain cachet she might not otherwise have had.'

Lil Wightman, owner of Le Louvre, the legendary Collins Street haute couture house, attended Cafe Florentino's 1928 opening and it remained her favourite restaurant until she died in 1993 aged ninety. As a working single mother, Lil arranged for her daughter, Georgina Weir, to entertain there before school dances and instructed Leon that Georgina was never to be presented with a bill, which should be forwarded instead to Le Louvre. Years later and well into her thirties, Georgina wondered about this and asked George why she had never had to pay. 'Oh, no,' he said. 'Strict instructions were left that you were never to receive a bill.'

Lil often had a 'nursery dinner' at 6.30 p.m. in the Restaurant, preceded by a whisky at Le Louvre, remembers Georgina. 'On Fridays she'd go with a pack of old cronies for lunch. They all drank brandy crustas, as you could tell from the coating of sugar around their mouths. One lunchtime Lady someone had a few too many and toppled off her chair into the aisle. Lil told the waiters to leave her there because she always did it, and there she stayed throughout lunch, with people hopping over and around her. Even more amazing, Mum made no attempt to rouse her when lunch was over and they all left.'

The restaurant wasn't expensive, according to George, who said he saw others in the area go broke charging high prices. 'If we were 70 per cent full for lunch, dinner was always busier, especially since the [nearby] Comedy, Princess and Her Majesty's were the only theatres then. When *My Fair Lady* opened we had more people than we could cope with, all dressed up and in a hurry, talking and moving from table to table. It was like a party.' There would be a full **pre-theatre service**, then a complete reset for dinner.

George was so successful that he repaid his loan by 1968 without ever needing to advertise for business – except in one special case. 'In the sixties it became fashionable for men to unbutton their shirts and wear jeans, and it was impossible,' said George. 'The other customers would object. I had a lot of "squares", but they were good customers. So I allowed casual dress in the old room only, but it was hard to control and I made a lot of enemies trying to police it.' Then, on a 1965 world trip, he discovered a particular wording used in an upmarket restaurant in Hawaii. Back in Melbourne he mentioned it to *Sun* newspaper columnist and regular patron Keith Dunstan. 'Underneath his column I asked him to write "At the Florentino a tie is requested, jacket required", no phone number, nothing else. It created a sensation. The *Herald* wrote an article about it that generated thousands of dollars' worth of publicity. All the advertising people who came to the restaurant were full of admiration.'

The rule soon hardened into 'no tie, no jacket, no entry' and extended even to the sartorial suitability of one's footwear. It turned the Mural Room into the holy of holies, with the head waiter presiding over lunch in a morning suit, and dinner in white tie and tails. There being no exceptions to the dress rule, it became the sport of certain individuals – cartoonist and food critic Peter Russell-Clarke was among the worst – to get past the head waiter on some pretext or other.

George was shrewd enough to keep the outside room less formal, giving patrons a reason to prefer it in its own right over the hallowed inside room, and staff devised their own ways of coping with the differences. The jacketless film reviewer Ivan Hutchinson, for example, became the reason why inside-room staff invested in spare jackets and ties when, arriving for lunch with Channel 7 boss Gordon French, Ivan's party – and their tips – were lost to the more relaxed outside room.

George also had a way of dealing with overly refreshed patrons, recalls Andy Sinn, a Florentino regular since the early 1960s. 'Before Podgornik's renovations, the staircase was straight and treacherous and there were many stories of people falling down them drunk,' he says. 'If someone became aggressive, George would coax them to the top of the stairs then walk down backwards – he was well practised – with both parties hurling abuse at each other as they went. When they reached the bottom, it wouldn't matter who they were – the doorman would open the door and out they'd go.'

Eric Page, the *Herald*'s food critic, was also shown the door when he fronted up after a bad review. George felt Page didn't understand Italian food, which was probably correct given that, although Italian food has since gone the distance, French cuisine was the benchmark then. The Florentino's stand-out dishes were the antipasto, the (French!) duck l'orange, saltimbocca and scaloppine marsala. The consistency of the minestrone was said to be unparalleled and Peter Rowland swore by George's bolognaise sauce, the secret of which, he says, was cloves. Chocolate soufflé was the dessert of choice but it went off at 9 p.m. because the kitchen closed half an hour later. > page 144

BELOW George Tsindos (left), whose involvement with the Florentino as employee and owner spanned fifty years, and his son, Raymond (right), with the restaurant's brigade of chefs in the mid-1970s.

I Murali

The nine murals that adorn the Restaurant were painted by Anne Montgomery, Walter Beaumont, Jeane Diamond and Colvin Smith, each working on individual panels. These artists were students of Mervyn Napier Waller, the 'mural king' whose allegorical works adorn also the Australian War Memorial, the Melbourne Town Hall, State Library of Victoria and Myer Mural Hall.

BELOW Detail from Panel 7 (see page 142).

OPPOSITE Colvin Smith's Panel 1 depicts Florence in the full flush of its Renaissance achievement and includes several leading political and artistic figures.

The panels feature prominent Tuscan Renaissance figures including painters da Vinci, Raphael, Botticelli, Giotto and Michelangelo; goldsmiths Ghiberti and Cellini; sculptor Donatello (Panel 1); writer Boccaccio, poet Dante and his subject Beatrice (Panel 3); and ruler Lorenzo the Magnificent (Waller's only contribution to the project) and Florentine nobles (Panel 2). Among the settings depicted are the towns of San Gimignano (Panel 7) and Fiesole (Panel 6), and the Ponte Vecchio in Florence (Panel 9).

The murals are mostly large and horizontal, painted in oils on canvas, but according to Leon Massoni they were intended as an architectural statement – to be read as part of the room, and not framed (as occurred during the 1989 renovations). George Tsindos said the panels were painted at Waller's Flinders Street studio and delivered to the back door of the Florentino on the Greek fruiterer's horse and dray.

Botticelli was renowned for portraying friends and family in his paintings of Florentine court and aristocracy. Tradition also has it that the blue-garbed female figure looking into the Florentino's inner sanctum from Panel 4 is Mary Reed, a friend of Colvin Smith and Walter Beaumont. Both men were in love with her, but she was interested in neither. Beaumont, who painted this panel, depicted himself as the young man gazing up at her, seemingly never to be satisfied. (For his part, Smith separately composed in her honour an 'Ode to a Reed on Whom I Never Played'.)

As well as providing a visual feast for generations of diners, the murals are now an attraction in their own right, not least because they epitomise a period of extravagant decoration before iconoclastic Modernism and functional architecture took hold. Italophile Gough Whitlam did not

encounter the murals until he became prime minister in 1972 and graduated from the Grill to the Mural Room. According to George Tsindos, an admiring Whitlam returned often after that, bringing parties of people to marvel at the works.

Despite being cleaned during the 1989 renovation, the murals had never been restored until a four-year project was commenced by the Grossi family and the University of Melbourne in 2003. One by one the panels are leaving the Mural Room for the first time since their installation, to return glowing with the original clear Tuscan hues that have been obscured for decades.

TOP Lorenzo de'Medici, Florence's uncrowned king and the fountainhead of the new culture that ignited the Italian Renaissance, is seen riding through the streets in Jeane Diamond's Panel 2.

CENTRE In Panel 1, artists gather in Piazza della Signora to decide the position of Michelangelo's *David*. Ghiberti is talking to Donatello and Luco della Robbia at left; Raphael, Michelangelo and Botticelli are in the centre; and Leonardo is to the right with Cellini, artist and ruffian, duelling behind him. The black-robed monk is Savonarola; Guelphs and Ghibellines fight in the background.

BOTTOM LEFT A party of nobles picnics on the outskirts of San Gimignano in Anne Montgomery's Panel 7. At right are peasants passing by on their way to market.

BOTTOM RIGHT A detail of Anne Montgomery's Panel 3 shows Giotto, as a young shepherd, drawing on stone slabs. Behind him is the Campanile, Giotto Tower, representing one phase of his genius. At right are Arnaldo de Cambro and Francesco Talenti, designer and builder of Florence's Duomo; and Brunelleschi, who was responsible for its great dome.

Photos: John Romeo

As a manager, George was tough but fair. On one occasion he became so agitated he instructed the staff, 'And when you talk to me, shut up!' It became a catchcry. George didn't talk much, but his eyes were everywhere and he missed nothing. New employees were subjected to his relentless attention until, after several weeks, they'd undertaken some sort of test and were invited either to leave or to stay, in which latter case he would leave them alone. Trevor York, who was head waiter from 1975 until the early 1980s, recalls his days dodging George as a junior waiter in 1969. One lunchtime Trevor was standing in the window when George boomed, 'What are you doing there? The customers are over here!' Another time he had three pens in his top pocket. 'You look like an out-of-work carpenter!' roared George. He took some getting used to, says Trevor, but then he *was* running a first-class establishment.

Then, as now, leading actors, singers and performers frequented the Restaurant. Shirley Bassey, Lauren Bacall, Charlton Heston, Phyllis Diller, Dame Joan Sutherland, Tony Martin, Spike Milligan and Harry Secombe are among those York served during his period of employ. Sammy Davis Jr came for lunch but didn't eat, preferring bourbon on the rocks. Leslie Caron and Louis Jourdan opted to share a table with Trevor York when, arriving late, they found him eating his own dinner.

Rudolf Nureyev was among the most playful guests. 'He came often with Dame Margot Fonteyn and Sir Robert Helpmann,' says Tony Rao, now Grossi Florentino's storeman. 'One night in the mid-seventies there were about ten of them in the inside room, including John-Michael Howson, celebrating Nureyev's birthday with a cake provided by the management. I was pouring the wine and Nureyev leaned towards me, gesturing with the cake trowel, and said in perfect Italian, "How would they feel if I put this up their arses?" Everyone wanted to know what he'd said. I replied that he was touched by the cake, and they all clapped.'

Around the same time, Roger Moore was in town for the Logies and came to dine in the inside room every night with the pilot of his private plane, smoking cigars and drinking Valpolicella (he was married to an Italian at the time). 'One night he was there and we were very busy,' recalls Rao. 'The head waiter said Rock Hudson [who was also in Melbourne for the Logies] was downstairs and we had to find a table quick.

Moore was finishing so we moved him on. The chair was still warm and they met on the stairs.' Also somewhat flummoxed was the tired and emotional lone diner on a neighbouring table. Having imbibed enough to request Moore's autograph, he later looked up to see Hudson sitting in the same spot. Once more he ventured forth, telling the new arrival that his predecessor had obliged him. 'I'm not Roger Moore,' was Hudson's less than gracious response.

Dame Joan Hammond lunched weekly in the 1970s; Olivia Newton-John, always with her back to the room and at Table 24, ate with Sir Philip Jones (then chairman of the Herald & Weekly Times Ltd; not to be confused with the writer Philip Jones) and his wife; and Barry Humphries is remembered by many a disgruntled waiter for always sitting with his long legs sticking out into the room.

It was in the 1970s also that property developer Floyd (Florian) Podgornik, a former carpenter born in Trieste of an Italian mother and Yugoslavian father, began frequenting the Restaurant. 'He didn't know what cutlery to use in the beginning and the wine was always "my usual",' says Rao. 'But he was very, very smart, very personable and a big tipper, so everyone made a fuss. He came in with [union leaders] Norm Gallagher and John Halfpenny and never had a strike on any of his building sites, so he knew where to put the oil.'

From the late 1970s and through the 1980s, Andy Sinn presided over Friday lunch at a round table at the top of the stairs in the outside room, joined by a movable feast of about ten male friends from the worlds of broking, banking, finance, law and fashion. 'We always did a deal with George (and, later, Branco) for a two-course lunch with wine for half the going rate, making a welter of drinking more than a bottle each,' says Sinn. The bill was settled with Rikki-Tikki, a game of bluff and elimination played by calling common numbers on bank notes. The last one left pays the bill – a shocking prospect after a long liquid lunch. 'You'd be shitting yourself at the end and then have to go to George or Branco to get credit.' This was always forthcoming for the regular 'family', and in the pre-computer era George operated exclusively on cash or monthly accounts anyway – about 2500 of them. He said he didn't want credit cards and worked that way to keep the place accessible to those without expense accounts. And he never lost one cent of money owed, even from companies that went broke.

BELOW **Branco Tocigl, who owned and operated the Florentino from 1980 until 1989.**

Photo: The Herald & Weekly Times Photographic Collection

ABOVE A painting of the Florentino as it looked when Branco Tocigl owned it in the 1980s, before the lavish 1989 renovation upgraded the exterior. From 1963 until 1979, while the Tsindos family was in charge, their surname was splashed across the facade.

By the time he decided to call it a day, George had been at the Florentino as waiter and owner for thirty-seven years, surviving three recessions. 'I told an agent I was thinking of selling, then changed my mind. But he could see I was running down and advised me to. Branco got it through him. I knew Branco because when I was in business in Sorrento I used to go to Mario's on Sunday nights, and he was the doorman. There was always a crowd but Branco would beckon me forward and let me in. When I told the staff I was going to sell, they were crying and I was crying, then I cried day and night for months. I'm not exaggerating.' Possibly he would have cried more had he known that on the night before handing over to Branco, his son Raymond invited some mates to the Restaurant and they drank Dom Perignon all night and cleaned out the bar.

George had bought the freehold for one building from Leon Massoni, the other from the Wynns, and he sold the lot to Branco Tocigl and three silent partners. They bought a gold mine, according to the staff. Branco took over on New Year's Day 1980, at the very beginning of the **decade of greed and excess**. One needed to book a week ahead for lunch and people queued on the stairs – the who's who of the day, including a cast of 1980s characters, such as Russ Hinze, Queensland's corpulent and controversial Police Minister. He prompted a modification of George's dress code when, seated by necessity at some distance from the table, he finished up with more spaghetti resting on his huge stomach than in it. After that, Branco introduced optional bibs.

But it was Robert Sangster's jacket – or lack thereof – that caused the greatest furore around the dress code. Drink waiter Mario Mocellin was there and says he copped the blame. It was Cup Eve 1987 and the city was sweltering in unseasonable 40-degree heat. As usual, the racing fraternity was celebrating at lunch, but the airconditioning couldn't cope and it became so hot that Nigel Dempster, the Australian-born English gossip columnist, stood up and said, 'Ladies and gentlemen, how about we break with tradition and take our coats off? Will you follow me?' And all the men did, including Sangster. He was just one of many, but as the owner of a Cup winner and former husband of Susan Rossiter-Peacock-Sangster-Renouf, possibly the best known. Mario was reprimanded, even though he'd done the right thing and referred Dempster to Branco's son Marco, who was in charge that day. The next day it was all over the papers and beaten up into a huge indiscretion. Branco was cross with Mario at the time but less so a few days later, when car dealer Reg Hunt congratulated him on all the free publicity.

Meanwhile, Peter Rowland found himself banned for a second time. He was at the Cup Eve lunch and, like every other male, removed his jacket. The next day he was summoned by Branco, who told him, 'Mr Peter, we very much appreciate your custom but from now on, stay downstairs.' Rowland asked why and was told it was because he had gone jacketless in the Mural Room. So did everyone else, Rowland protested. 'Yes,' said Branco, 'but you're the only one I know.' Rowland told him he was an idiot and kept frequenting the Mural Room, where to this day he often wears a dinner jacket because he feels comfortable thus attired in that setting.

In those days before the Fringe Benefits Tax (FBT), when restaurant meals were still deductible, the Florentino was always full to bursting. People like Sir Eric Pearce, Sir Rod Carnegie, Sir Cecil Looker, Lindsay Fox, Ron Walker and Lloyd Williams almost lived there. Celebrated criminal lawyer Frank Galbally arrived accompanied always by a small, dark man in a camel-hair coat, a 'Siciliano' who staff fantasised, maybe correctly, was his bodyguard. They all trusted the waiters to take care of the bill and add their own tips. Long lunches were the norm at which Dom Perignon flowed until 4 and 5 p.m. in some cases, with at least a third of the clientele staying on into the afternoon to talk business.

Graham Kennedy, a fan since the days when he had given Flo's free plugs on Channel 9's *In Melbourne Tonight*, returned often for his favourite waiters and the food, which he ate, usually alone, with a napkin tucked into his shirt collar, and always left a generous tip. For Bert Newton, it was the setting for school reunions with a Father Joe from Brunswick and an air force officer. Around 3.30 p.m. departing staff would tell them to help themselves to the fridge, and by 6 p.m., when the staff returned, the table would be full of empty stubbies.

In the pre-fax and email 1980s, socialite Sheila Scotter kept up with the Italian-based Australian painter Jeffrey Smart at infrequent lunch dates. Returning to Australia every year or two, he would telegram ahead, 'Lunch please [followed by the date] usual place usual time unusual love Smart.' The usual place, as Scotter knew, was a table window in the inside room; the time, one o'clock. And one of the noisiest nights of those

147

flamboyant times was when the polo-playing 61st Indian Cavalry came to dinner and finished up standing on the chairs to demonstrate their winning shots.

Branco was a gracious and generous host throughout, and his presence at the top of the stairs set the tone, says Andy Sinn. He was always a soft touch for charity and would pick up the bill for the regulars' birthday dinners. Times were good and employees were indulged at lavish Christmas parties. One of these parties, to which Branco bussed the entire staff and their families, was at the Mitchelton winery and cost $25 000.

But the 1980s came to an abrupt end for the restaurant trade when the federal Labor Government introduced the FBT in mid-1985. It cut the Restaurant's lunch trade from 38 to about 10 tables, although some regulars did opt for the cheaper Grill or Cellar Bar. A few weeks after the tax came in, long-time waiter Marcello Bidese served leading Liberals Andrew Peacock and Ian Macphee at their usual Table 25 in the almost-empty inside room. Peacock asked Marcello what he thought of the tax. 'Between Paul Cheating [Treasurer Paul Keating] and Don Potato Chips [Democrat leader Don Chipp, who supported the FBT], they've closed us up,' he told them. Business did recover once people got used to the new tax, but it took a couple of years and never returned to the halcyon days of the 1970s and early 1980s.

By 1989 Branco was in poor health, and Floyd Podgornik, the patron who had said he loved Cafe Florentino so much he would have to buy it, did just that. He embarked immediately on a **grand restoration and redesign**, closing the business for several months and provoking an outcry from the press, the patrons and Melburnians in general, who regarded the Florentino as an institution, if not a sacred site. In May 1989 the National Trust and the Historic Building Council called a halt to the renovations while they reviewed the building's registration, confined originally to the Mural Room.

Podgornik did much necessary wiring, plumbing and structural work – virtually the first such work since Rinaldo's day – but his renovations called for one large bistro area, with the staircase removed to one side and a virtual gutting of the downstairs area. In the eventual compromise the original Bistro Grill went but the Cellar Bar was retained and refurbished, the central staircase was redesigned to include a landing, and

ABOVE **Guy Grossi searched high and low for a suitable cheese cabinet before he found this old shop-display unit among a restorer's junk, and had it refurbished.**

ABOVE **Lorraine Podgornik (left), proprietor of the Florentino from 1990 to 1999, with regular patron Lillian Frank.**
Photo: Josh Ellis

the upstairs rooms were redecorated. Floyd removed an ugly partition, restoring the Restaurant to the way it had looked in Rinaldo's day, installed black marble bathrooms and employed young artists to remove the grime from the murals. He then added seventeenth-century chandeliers and 24-carat gold leaf to the ceilings.

When Cafe Florentino reopened in November 1989 it was still recognisably Australia's oldest first-class restaurant, but it had had a first-class facelift. Leon Massoni declared it a triumph and says that only someone in the building business could have afforded to do it. He claims that Podgornik and Max Moar, the developer of the Grand Hyatt, were in competition to achieve the best result. The staff, most of whom stayed on, were certainly happy, as Floyd had been a valued and popular customer. His girlfriend, Carolyn Palliardi, was nominally in charge and is remembered by staff as being so timid she would chat endlessly with them rather than venture into the Restaurant.

It all came to an abrupt end within five months when Floyd suicided in March 1990. In the public dispute that ensued between Carolyn and Floyd's widow, Lorraine, the latter emerged with control of the Florentino and literally walked through the front door as Carolyn exited into the back lane. Lorraine soon had cause to reflect on what she'd been so keen to acquire, as businesses everywhere suffered in the **worsening recession**. Many regulars had moved to the Latin during the renovations and not all of them returned. The Restaurant had been unfavourably reviewed under Floyd and a lot of people weren't happy with the changes. Besides, Lorraine wasn't a restaurateur and had no idea of the Florentino's institutional status, history and clientele. She'd eaten there rarely and then only in the Bistro Grill. 'I remember being quite overwhelmed and concerned about how I was going to manage, but I never thought of not giving it a go,' says Lorraine. 'Staff morale was low and they were all quite worried about their jobs and the future, so it was quite scary.'

She invited Peter Rowland to run the business (which he did for almost two years) and went in every day and night, always in the background learning and listening. Above all she learned discretion, and remembers being firmly nudged by the head waiter as they stood together at the top of the stairs one night, about to greet a patron who'd dined the previous evening with a different woman. ('Unofficial' couples are part of the delicious pot of restaurant life, says Rowland, who has been witness to generations of rich and well-known older men entertaining gorgeous young women at the Florentino.) All the long-serving staff stayed on, so there was continuity.

Once people realised that Lorraine was definitely there for the very long haul, old regulars started coming back, she says. 'It was a difficult time and a huge challenge, and I could have sold the business many, many times. There wasn't one Melbourne restaurateur who didn't want it. But my biggest lesson was that the Florentino doesn't ever belong to you – you share it. The owner might have all the responsibility but when it comes to changes, even something as simple as the napkins, everyone has a view.'

The Restaurant had never won a culinary award and, when Lorraine inquired, she was told this was because the *Age Good Food Guide* editors considered it 'an institution'. During her time it won a coveted chef's hat four years running and a new American Express award for Waiter of the Year.

By 1999 Lorraine was ready to trade a full-time commitment and big responsibility for more personal time. 'I became very friendly with people and they always wanted me there, but I got to the stage of wanting to travel more,' she says. Guy Grossi had already approached her and since, deep down, she wanted the business to go to a family who would put their heart and soul into it, she and Guy did a deal.

BELOW Guy Grossi, owner/chef of Grossi Florentino since 1999.

Thus began the current era. The Grossi family took over in March 1999, and under their control the Restaurant has undergone a renaissance at every level. It has regained its place as Melbourne's leading Italian restaurant, with accolades and three chef's hats attesting to the first-class quality of the food and service. Every detail is finessed, from the standard of tableware to the original dining chairs, now refurbished with leather Italian-style as in Rinaldo's day.

Reinvigorated, Cafe Florentino – now Grossi Florentino – continues into the new millennium with a clientele that reads like the invitation list to a convention of entrepreneurs, business leaders, powerbrokers and celebrities. It's where Chris Corrigan lunched with Sir Richard Branson when Corrigan's Patrick Corporation bought an interest in Branson's Virgin Blue airline, for example.

And other things don't change either. Not so long ago an older man and a younger woman arrived by limousine for a late lunch. She was an attractive brunette (a 'cappuccino type', according to Guy, who was in the Wynn Room writing menus when they walked in) wearing a fetching halter-neck top. Suddenly Guy became aware of various staff members streaming up the stairs, allegedly seeking supplies. It seems that the young woman's companion had asked the waiter, 'Do you mind if my girlfriend shows me her tits?' The waiter had shrugged in the Italian manner of expressing surprise and, taking that as a no, the woman dropped her top. Only one table of businessmen remained in the Mural Room and they'd already asked for their bill. Immediately they ordered another bottle of wine and, after much shared laughter and many drinks with their new friends, the couple departed as they'd arrived.

RIGHT During a first-class dining experience, women shouldn't be expected to leave their handbags on the floor. At Grossi Florentino, fittingly, they can rest their bags on these fabric-covered stands, an idea Guy Grossi took from an up-market restaurant in Paris.

Grissini all'oliva – Olive-flavoured breadsticks

This recipe is not complicated, but it is a bit fiddly and time and patience are required. *Grissini* taste fresh and delicious, and presenting them at the table adds an air of care for the diner and attention to detail. I believe they are worth the time it takes to make them. ∼ *Makes approximately 25*

2 teaspoons fresh yeast

125 ml warm water

pinch of caster sugar

approximately 750 g flour

¼ cup kalamata olives, pitted

sea salt

Preheat the oven to 170°C. Lightly grease 2–3 baking trays. Combine the yeast with a little of the warm water, add the sugar and a pinch of the flour and mix until smooth. Set aside in a warm place to prove for 10 minutes.

Purée the olives in a blender and transfer to a mixing bowl with 5 teaspoons of sea salt and the remaining flour. Tip in the yeast mixture and mix well with a wooden spoon. Add the remaining warm water a little at a time. Test the consistency – it should be firm but not too dry, and should come away from the sides of the bowl. Add more water, if required. Form into a large ball.

Sprinkle some flour on your work surface. Using a rolling pin or a pasta machine, roll out the dough to a thickness of about 3 mm and cut into 25 cm × 1 cm strips. Transfer to the baking trays, sprinkle with sea salt and bake (in batches, if necessary) for 15–20 minutes or until golden brown. Break one open to see whether it is dry on the inside – if so, remove the trays from the oven. Cool. The *grissini* will keep for 1 week in an airtight container in a cool, dry place.

Tagliarini con riccio di mare – Tagliarini with sea urchin

The only edible part of a sea urchin is the orange-red bands (called 'coral') that cling to the insides of the spiny shell. Although there is very little of it, the flavour is extremely memorable. It is the flavour of the ocean! ∾ *Bottarga*, or sun-dried mullet roe, is a delicacy from Sardinia and Sicily. The roe (eggs) of the fish are dried while still in their sacs, and the finished product comes in long, narrow oval shapes. I was ecstatic when I found that a local version was being made in Queensland, and have been using it ever since. I found it in the deli section at David Jones, when I was shopping with the family. For imported Sardinian *bottarga*, try a specialist Italian food store. ∾ *Serves 4*

2 large sea urchins

500 g pasta dough (see page 217)

olive oil

2 cloves garlic, thinly sliced

1 chilli, seeded and finely sliced

1 tablespoon pesto (see page 36)

20 g finely chopped flat-leaf parsley

25 g bottarga (sun-dried mullet roe), crushed

¼ cup freshly chopped oregano

sea salt and freshly ground black pepper

Using a tea towel, hold a sea urchin in your hand and put the tip of a pair of pliers into the underside or concave side of the creature. Break the shell gently, working your way around until all the urchin roe is exposed. Gently dislodge the roe and put it on a tray. Repeat with the other sea urchin.

Roll out the pasta dough on a floured surface, then fold through a pasta machine until well laminated. Roll out the dough to a thickness of about 3 mm and roll up the sheet into a log. Using a sharp knife, cut fine ribbons of pasta (these are the *tagliarini*). Cook in a large pot of salted boiling water until al dente.

Meanwhile, heat the olive oil in a frying pan and sauté the garlic, chilli, pesto, parsley and bottarga. Add the sea urchin roe and cook quickly. Drain the pasta, toss through the contents of the frying pan and serve immediately.

Ravioli di scampi in brodino di aragosta – Scampi ravioli poached in rock lobster broth, with chicory and lemon-thyme sabayon

Scampi are crustaceans with a more delicate flavour and texture than prawns or rock lobster. In Australia they are generally available frozen, imported from New Zealand. Scampi have always had a place in Italian menus in pasta and risotto or, of course, lightly battered and fried. This dish dresses them up in pasta and their flavour is intensified by cooking them in broth, not water. The dandelion chicory (*Cichorium intybus*) adds a welcome bitter twist. ᔕ *Serves 4*

8 large scampi, shelled but with tails left on

freshly ground black pepper

¼ cup freshly chopped flat-leaf parsley

¼ cup freshly chopped dill

100 g butter

2 cloves garlic, chopped

1 teaspoon freshly chopped ginger

1 bay leaf

sea salt

1 leek, finely sliced and well washed

1 small bulb fennel, finely sliced and well washed

500 g pasta dough (see page 217)

leaves from 250 g dandelion chicory, washed

To make the rock lobster broth (ingredients opposite), put the olive oil, onion, carrot, celery, bay leaves, peppercorns and fennel powder in a medium-sized pot and cook for a few minutes until soft. Add the lobster shells and mix well. Cook briefly until the shells are toasted, then crush (still in the pot) with a mallet. Cover with water and simmer for about 2 hours. Strain through a fine sieve and keep warm.

Season the scampi with pepper, parsley and dill and set aside. Melt half the butter in a pot and add the garlic, ginger and bay leaf, and salt and pepper to taste. Add the leek and fennel and cook gently for 5 minutes, stirring, until soft but not coloured. Allow to cool.

Using a pasta machine or rolling pin, roll out the pasta dough and cut into 8 cm squares. Put a little fennel mixture in the centre of each square and then put a scampi on top, so that the tail protrudes from the edge of the dough. Fold the dough over the filling, wet the edges and press together well,

ROCK LOBSTER BROTH

100 ml olive oil

1 small onion, roughly chopped

1 carrot, roughly chopped

1 stalk celery, roughly chopped

2 bay leaves

4 black peppercorns

1 teaspoon roasted fennel powder

500 g rock lobster shells (available from your fishmonger)

LEMON-THYME SABAYON

2 egg yolks

leaves from 2 sprigs lemon thyme

125 ml verjuice

sea salt and freshly ground black pepper

particularly around the scampi tail. It should look as if the scampi is trying to 'crawl into' the pasta. Trim the edges neatly. Bring the lobster broth to the boil in a large pot and poach the ravioli for 4 minutes. Melt the remaining butter in a pan and sauté the chicory leaves, seasoning to taste with salt and pepper. Mix in the drained ravioli.

To make the sabayon, put the egg yolks in a double boiler with the other ingredients. Whisk constantly over a low heat for a few minutes, so that air is incorporated into the yolks and the sabayon becomes light and foamy. To serve, put 2 ravioli in the middle of each plate so that one is resting on the other. Arrange some chicory leaves around and drizzle sabayon around the plate and over the ravioli.

Tortellini di anatra e funghi con pera – Duck and wild mushroom tortellini with caramelised pear

I am often asked, 'What is your signature dish?' I find it difficult to choose, but this would have to be a contender. The flavours of the roasted duck and mushroom marry so well, and the sweetness of the pear enhances the experience. ∾ Durum wheat semolina is a yellow flour used for making pasta. We grow our own in Australia and it can now be found in good supermarkets. It is not to be confused with semolina, which is a different product and no good for pasta. ∾ *Serves 6*

125 ml olive oil

1 onion, roughly chopped

1 carrot, roughly chopped

2 stalks celery, roughly chopped

1 × 2.2 kg duck

sea salt and freshly ground black pepper

1 teaspoon freshly crushed rosemary

1 teaspoon juniper berries, crushed

200 g tomato paste

750 ml red wine

125 g flour

125 g durum wheat semolina

2 eggs

butter

Preheat the oven to 180ºC. Put the olive oil, onion, carrot and celery in a roasting tray and rest the duck on top. Season well with salt and pepper, rosemary and juniper and drizzle with some more oil. Roast until well cooked, about 45 minutes. Allow to cool a little, then take the meat off the bones and set it aside. Return the bones to the oven and allow to deepen in colour for 15 minutes. Tip the contents of the roasting tray into a large pot, add the tomato paste and wine and bring to the boil. Boil for 10 minutes, then cover with water and simmer gently for 3 hours. Strain through a fine sieve. Discard the bones and transfer the liquid to a small saucepan. Reduce until rich and glossy, with the consistency of olive oil.

To make the filling (ingredients on page 160), heat the olive oil in a heavy-based saucepan and sauté the onion and garlic until soft. Add the reserved duck meat, the herbs and the mushrooms. Stir in the tomato paste, marsala and stock, and cook for 10 minutes until well combined. Allow to cool, >

159

DUCK AND WILD MUSHROOM FILLING

50 ml olive oil

1 onion, chopped

1 clove garlic, sliced

meat from the roasted duck (see method), roughly chopped

½ cup freshly chopped flat-leaf parsley

½ teaspoon freshly chopped sage

300 g wild mushrooms, soaked and chopped

2 tablespoons tomato paste

100 ml marsala

200 ml chicken stock (see page 215)

2 eggs

¼ cup grated Parmigiano-Reggiano

sea salt and freshly ground black pepper

CARAMELISED PEAR

1 large, firm pear, peeled, cored and cut into 1 cm cubes

6 tablespoons brown sugar

200 ml white wine

then mince (do not blend or purée). Transfer to the bowl of an electric mixer and, using a large paddle on a slow speed, add the eggs and Parmigiano-Reggiano to taste. Season with salt and pepper and mix until firm but moist.

Mix the flour, semolina and eggs and knead until smooth and elastic. Fold the dough into a pasta machine and continue to roll and fold through the machine at least 15 times to 'laminate' the pasta. Roll out thinly and cut out approximately 60 circles 7–8 cm in diameter. Put a small amount of filling in the centre of each circle and fold the circle in half, then take the two corners, curl the pasta towards you and press the ends together to join.

To make the caramelised pear, put the pear and brown sugar in a frying pan over moderate heat. Add the wine and simmer slowly until the sugar caramelises.

Cook the tortellini in a large pot of boiling salted water for 4–5 minutes. Drain. Toss with the caramelised pear and a little butter, drizzle the duck sauce over and serve.

Terrina di salmone – Atlantic salmon terrine

This terrine is as pleasing to the eye as it is to the tastebuds, and really showcases the freshness of the ingredients. The *scapece* sauce is a traditional method of treating fish with sweet and sour flavours, while the saffron provides a brilliant colour contrast. Tasmanian Atlantic salmon is my choice for this dish; I enjoy working with such a world-class product. ❧ *Serves 6–8*

1 Atlantic salmon fillet, skinned and boned

1 litre duck fat (available from poultry suppliers)

20 large scallops (without roe), cleaned

12 large cos lettuce leaves

6 large Roma tomatoes, cored

50 g freshly chopped mixed herbs (choose from oregano, basil, chervil, dill, flat-leaf parsley and coriander)

sea salt

handful of capers

olive oil

handful of pomegranate seeds

Preheat the oven to very low (50–70°C). Trim the salmon so it will fit into a 16 cm long × 7 cm deep terrine mould. Put the duck fat in a baking tray and melt over a low heat. Add the salmon and scallops, submerging them in the fat. Cover with foil and bake for 20–30 minutes with the oven door slightly open.

Blanch the cos leaves in boiling water for 5–10 seconds and refresh in cold water. Score the skins of the tomatoes and blanch them in boiling water for 20 seconds. Refresh in cold water, peel, quarter and remove the seeds.

Line your terrine mould with plastic wrap, then line with the wilted cos leaves so that when you fill the mould you will be able to wrap the leaves over the top. Remove the scallops from the fat and season with salt and pepper. Arrange tightly side by side in the mould. Put the tomato on top of the scallops and sprinkle over the herbs. Carefully remove the salmon from the fat and put it in the mould in one piece – you may need to use a spatula, as it will be very fragile. Fold the cos leaves over the top and cover with plastic wrap. Lay a heavy object on top to add pressure, and refrigerate overnight.

To make the relish (ingredients on page 162), deep-fry the eggplant in olive oil until golden brown and drain on kitchen paper. Heat a little more olive oil >

EGGPLANT RELISH

2 medium eggplants, cut into
5 mm batons

olive oil

2 shallots, sliced

1 clove garlic, finely chopped

100 g brown sugar

50 ml sherry vinegar

SCAPECE

50 ml olive oil

6 shallots, finely sliced

2 cloves

1 bay leaf

8 strands of saffron

20 g caster sugar

200 ml white wine

50 ml white-wine vinegar

in a separate pot and sauté the shallots and garlic until just coloured. Stir in the brown sugar and let it caramelise. Deglaze the pot with the sherry vinegar and simmer for 2 minutes. Gently mix in the eggplant and set aside to cool. (The relish will keep for up to 3 days in the refrigerator.)

To make the *scapece*, heat the olive oil in a pot and add the shallot, cloves and bay leaf. Cook gently over a moderate heat for 5 minutes or until the shallot softens but does not take on any colour. Stir in the saffron strands and caster sugar, then deglaze the pot with the wine and vinegar and simmer for 5 minutes. Cool. (The *scapece* will keep for up to 3 days in the refrigerator.)

To serve, cut the terrine into 2 cm slices. Spoon some eggplant relish onto the centre of each plate and, using a spatula, put a slice of terrine on top. Spoon some *scapece* around the outside and scatter with flakes of sea salt, capers fried in a little hot olive oil, and pomegranate seeds.

Risotto con aragosta, Bellavista e zucchini – Risotto with rock lobster, Bellavista sparkling wine and zucchini

Risotto is from the *cucina* of northern Italy. There is an infinite number of risotto recipes; this one makes use of some indulgent ingredients, including rock lobster, Bellavista sparkling wine and saffron – a great combination that produces a special dish. ∾ Bellavista is considered Italy's best sparkling wine and equal to the great French champagnes. The vineyard is located in the picturesque Franciacorta region of Lombardia, east of Milan. ∾ *Serves 4*

1 × 800 g rock lobster

butter

6 shallots, finely chopped

1 clove garlic, chopped

pinch of saffron

¼ cup freshly chopped dill

1 bay leaf

400 g superfine arborio rice

30 ml Bellavista sparkling wine
(*or* other dry sparkling wine)

1–1.5 litres rock lobster broth
(see page 157)

1 zucchini, cut into 1 cm dice

olive oil

sea salt and freshly ground black pepper

25 g freshly grated Parmigiano-Reggiano

If the lobster is still alive, drown it in a bucket of cold, fresh water for 15 minutes. Bring a large pot of water to the boil, tip in the lobster and cook for approximately 10 minutes. Remove from the heat and put the pot under cold running water until the lobster has cooled completely. Twist the head and tail in opposite directions. Remove the tail fins and gently break the shell around them, trying not to break off or tear any of the flesh. Slice the lobster tail into 5 mm medallions. Separate the top from the bottom of the body, remove the legs and break open the joints where the legs meet the body. Pick the meat out of the joints and then break open the legs to get all the meat out. Using a mallet, break open the antennae to get the meat from them. Set all the meat aside. (Freeze the shells for later use in a bisque or broth – see pages 157 and 171.)

Melt 20 g butter in a pot. Add the shallot, garlic, saffron, dill and bay leaf and fry until soft. Add the rice and cook for 2–3 minutes – it will become slightly whiter. Deglaze the pot with the sparkling wine and add one-third of the rock lobster broth. Cook gently, stirring, and when the liquid has been absorbed, add another cup of broth. Continue this process for 20 minutes.

In a frying pan, sauté the zucchini in 20 g butter until light golden. Add the reserved lobster meat and toss together. Transfer the lobster and zucchini to the risotto pot and season to taste. Add 100 g butter and the Parmigiano-Reggiano, being sure to stir constantly. The end product should be thick and creamy, but still runny. If necessary, add some extra broth to loosen it a little. Serve immediately.

La Festa

In Italian, *festa* means everything from a feast to a party, holiday, festivity or entertainment. Italians love celebrating almost as much as they love eating, and every birthday, saint's day, family event or run-of-the-mill get-together is turned into an excuse for fun, feasting and festivities. So it's hardly surprising that when it comes to celebrating, generations of Melburnians have regarded Florentino as the place to party. Everything about it shrieks 'special occasion'.

Some diners – like Andy Sinn, who has probably eaten more meals at the Florentino than at home, including numerous birthday and New Year's Eve dinners – even find their way onto the menu. Aragosta alla Andrea (Lobster Mornay à la Andrew), now a fixture, was conceived by Guy Grossi for Sinn's 60th birthday – a memorable festa for eighty in the Mural Room, commencing with pre-lunch drinks in the Wynn Room and finishing at midnight.

In 1997, when Michael Zifcak of the Hill of Content commemorated the bookshop's 75th anniversary, he booked out the whole restaurant and invited 350 publishers, retailers and customers to a cocktail party. Among them was John Button, a patron of both establishments, who pointed out in his celebratory speech that Zifcak had only to punch a door in his office wall to reach his favourite table in the Mural Room window.

For some, the Florentino is a magical ingredient in their marriage. Couples joke that they stay married in anticipation of celebrating anniversaries in the Restaurant. Socialite Lillian Frank says her husband, Richard, took her there on one of their first dates; walking up the stairs was one of the most fantastic experiences of her young life. Ron Walker recalls it as the place to take girls he wanted to impress, in which circumstances George Tsindos would give him up to ninety days' credit. These days, Christmas Eve and Ron's wife Barbara's birthday are always celebrated there.

Weddings, private dinner parties, the annual unveiling of the Melbourne Cup by its makers, Hardy Brothers, and special musical and cultural dinners celebrating the Restaurant's history all feature. But the

OPPOSITE **Festive times at Grossi Florentino, clockwise from large picture: The main entrance dressed up for the Spring Racing Carnival; the Melbourne Cup and associated trophies; a publicity shot for the Florentino's 75th anniversary; long-time regular Andy Sinn (right) at his 60th birthday party (photo by Patrick Sinn).**

Happy 75th Birthday

GROSSI
FLORENTINO

Florentino's biggest annual festa and one of the most prominent on Melbourne's social calendar is the Cup Eve lunch, patronised by local, interstate and overseas racehorse owners, identities and trainers, socialites and their spouses, many of whom book from year to year. Tradition has it that the men lunch at tables for ten in the Mural Room, while the women hold court in the Wynn Room. These days there is some blurring of the lines because, as Andy Sinn says, there are always some girls who want to be in the boys' room and vice versa.

Interstate Cup Week visitors looking for some action between the Saturday Derby, the Sunday round of private parties and polo, and the Tuesday Cup were the original catalyst for the Cup Eve event, but Sinn was an early enthusiast. He's had the same table in the right-hand corner of the Wynn Room (always with the 'girls' and with an emphasis on female guests) for several decades, and is responsible for enlivening the lunch with traditional Italian songs. Soon after Branco Tocigl took over, the new owner included a

one-man band in New Year's Eve festivities, which was an opportunity for Sinn to prevail on Mario Mocellin (formerly one of Mario's famous singing waiters) to sing a few songs. Thereafter he insisted that Mocellin perform at functions like Cup Eve, where Sinn would introduce him.

'Mario would stand on a chair, arms akimbo – it was the highlight of the afternoon,' says Sinn. Mario became so popular that Peter Rowland hired him to perform at his private parties. Before long, food waiter Marcello Bidese joined in to sing duets, and everything would stop on Cup Eve for their renditions of 'O Sole Mio' and 'Torna a Surriento'. On occasion Susan Renouf got up on a chair and sang with them, as did John Elliott (sounding like Louis Armstrong, apparently) and Lillian and Richard Frank.

Now in their seventies and retired, the singing waiters have been replaced – but the Cup Eve lunch traditions continue, with a professional musical trio and an indefatigable group of what Rowland calls 'festa types' or 'funsters'.

Barramundi con brioche – Barramundi with a brioche crust

At the Restaurant we use wild barramundi, which is classed as a freshwater fish even though it travels downstream to seawater estuaries to breed. It has meaty flesh and a great flavour without being too 'muddy'. ∾ Brioche, obtainable at good bakeries and pastry shops, is only lightly sweetened and can therefore be used in savoury dishes. ∾ *Serves 4*

600 g kipfler potatoes, peeled

2 cloves garlic, peeled

¼ cup freshly chopped sage

50 g speck, diced

olive oil

4 × 250 g barramundi fillets

sea salt and freshly ground black pepper

flour

BRIOCHE CRUST

200 g brioche

50 g freshly chopped flat-leaf parsley

1 teaspoon cardamom powder

50 g walnuts

100 g softened butter

sea salt and freshly ground black pepper

To make the brioche crust, put the brioche, parsley, cardamom and walnuts into a food processor. Process, gradually adding the butter, until well incorporated. Season to taste, then set aside.

To make the bisque (ingredients opposite), sauté the onion, carrot, celery, leek and garlic in a little olive oil for a few minutes. Add the prawn shells and sauté until they are slightly coloured. Add the tomato paste and stir until it has taken on a little colour, then add the brandy, white wine and bay leaf. Bring to the boil and reduce by half. Pour in the water and return to the boil. Turn down the heat and simmer for 45 minutes until again reduced by half. Strain into a clean pot and add the cream. Reduce until thick but still runny, then pass through a fine sieve.

Preheat the oven to 200°C. Cut the potatoes in half lengthways and put them in a roasting tray with the garlic, sage and speck. Drizzle with 100 ml olive oil and bake for 20 minutes, turning occasionally, until golden brown. Season the barramundi with salt and pepper, dust with flour and shake off the excess. Heat a little olive oil in a pan and fry the fish flesh-side down for 2–3 minutes until golden brown. Turn over and repeat for the skin side.

PRAWN BISQUE

1 onion, chopped

1 carrot, chopped

1 stalk celery, chopped

1 leek, chopped

1 clove garlic, chopped

olive oil

400 g prawn *or* rock lobster shells
(available from your fishmonger)

50 g tomato paste

30 ml brandy

250 ml white wine

1 bay leaf

750 ml water

30 ml cream

Transfer to a baking dish and spread a thin layer of brioche crust on each fillet. Bake at 200°C for 10 minutes.

To serve, put some of the roasted potato, sage and speck in the middle of each plate. Set a barramundi fillet on top, crust-side up, and drizzle some bisque around.

Insalata di aragosta – Salad of rock lobster, Russian salad, watercress and beetroot jus

The strong, salty flavour of *bottarga* (see page 155) packs a punch and suits our rock lobster salad very well, while the sweetness of the beetroot jus cuts through the mayonnaise. Quail eggs are readily available from poultry suppliers. ❧ *Serves 6*

2 rock lobsters

1 beetroot, peeled and diced

60 ml white-wine *or* chardonnay vinegar

70 g caster sugar

½ cup watercress sprigs

6 quail eggs

white vinegar

12 slices bottarga (sun-dried mullet roe)

olive oil

RUSSIAN SALAD

6 large Spunta potatoes (*or* other variety)

1 large carrot, peeled and diced

1 cup peas

250 ml good-quality mayonnaise (see page 214)

3 teaspoons grated horseradish

sea salt and freshly ground black pepper

If you are using live lobsters, drown them in fresh iced water for 15 minutes before cooking. Bring to the boil a pot of water that is large enough to fit the 2 lobsters. Cook the lobsters for 10 minutes. (If you prefer, you can purchase 2 cooked lobsters from your fishmonger.) Meanwhile, start making the Russian salad by peeling the potatoes and putting them in a pot of cold water. Bring to the boil, reduce the heat and cook until the potatoes are soft but not falling apart. Add the carrot and peas about 5 minutes before the potatoes are ready. Drain and allow to cool completely.

Remove the lobster pot from the heat and put it under cold running water until the lobsters have cooled completely. Twist the head and tail of each lobster in opposite directions. Remove the tail fins and gently break the shell around them, trying not to break off or tear any of the flesh. Slice the lobster tail into 5 mm medallions. Separate the top from the bottom of the body, remove the legs and break open the joints where the legs meet the body. Pick the meat out of the joints and then break open the legs and extract the meat. Using a mallet, break open the antennae to get the meat from them. Set all the meat aside. (Freeze the shells for later use in a bisque or broth – see pages 157 and 171.) >

173

Put the beetroot in a small pot with the wine vinegar and sugar and cook until tender. Pick off about 30 sprigs of watercress, wash thoroughly and drain. Gently crack 1 quail egg into a cup, taking care not to break the yolk. Half-fill a small frying pan with water, add a splash of white vinegar and bring to the boil. Reduce the heat until barely simmering and, using a slotted spoon, swirl the water around to make a whirlpool. Tip in the egg and cook for 2 minutes. Remove and drain on kitchen paper. Keep warm while you repeat with the other eggs.

To finish making the Russian salad, cut the potatoes into small dice about the same size as the carrot. Mix with the carrot, peas, mayonnaise and horseradish, and season to taste with salt and pepper. You may need to add a little more mayonnaise if the mixture is too dry.

To serve, spoon some Russian salad into the centre of each plate. On top of this put some lobster meat from the legs. Arrange a few slices of tail meat on top, then a quail egg and 2 slices of bottarga. Drizzle some beetroot reduction around the plate, scatter over a few watercress sprigs and drizzle with a little olive oil.

Gamberi con crosta di erbe e orzo – Prawns with a herb crust and barley

Barley is so underused, yet is a wonderful grain that adds bite. I love it in salads and soups. It lends great texture to this dish and mops up the richness of the belly pork. The pork itself provides an interesting contrast to the flesh of the prawns. ❧ *Serves 4*

olive oil *or* vegetable oil

1 small onion, finely diced

1 small carrot, finely diced

1 stalk celery, finely diced

1 clove garlic, chopped

100 g speck, finely diced

250 g barley

seeds from 1 vanilla bean

500 ml chicken stock (see page 215)

sea salt and freshly ground black pepper

1 beetroot, peeled

8 prawns, peeled and deveined

CHIVE SAUCE

olive oil

1 small onion, diced

1 clove garlic, chopped

1 cup freshly chopped chives

500 ml chicken stock (see page 215)

Heat 50 ml olive oil in a large pot. Add the onion, carrot, celery, garlic and speck and fry together for 2–3 minutes. Mix in the barley and the vanilla seeds, pour in the stock and simmer gently for 20 minutes until the stock has been absorbed. Season to taste.

To make the chive sauce, heat a little olive oil in a pot and sauté the onion, garlic and half the chives until soft but not coloured. Add the chicken stock and simmer for 10 minutes. Stir in the remaining chives and cook for a further minute, then purée. Pass through a fine strainer. The colour will be vibrant.

To make the marinated belly pork (ingredients on page 176), mix the honey, garlic, chilli, salt, pepper and olive oil in a flat ceramic or glass dish. Marinate the pork for 2 hours. Preheat the oven to 180°C. Scatter the onion, carrot and celery in a roasting pan and put the pork on top, skin-side up. Pour over the marinade and roast for 30 minutes. Slice the pork thinly.

Slice the beetroot paper-thin across the bulb, then cut the slices into very thin strips. Heat 500 ml oil in a deep frying pan and deep-fry the beetroot for 5–10 seconds. Drain and cool on kitchen paper. >

MARINATED BELLY PORK

2 teaspoons honey

2 cloves garlic, chopped

1 chilli, seeded and chopped

sea salt and freshly ground black pepper

200 ml olive oil

200 g belly pork

1 small onion, chopped

1 carrot, chopped

1 stalk celery, chopped

HERB CRUST

2 cups cubed brioche

1 clove garlic, chopped

40 g freshly chopped flat-leaf parsley

grated zest of $\frac{1}{2}$ lemon

50–80 g softened butter

Preheat your grill to hot or the oven to 180°C. Lightly grease an oven tray with oil. To make the herb crust, blend the brioche, garlic, parsley and lemon zest to a fine consistency in a food processor. Add the butter a little at a time until you have a mixture that is pliable but not too soft. Make a small incision in the belly of each prawn and open it out. Fill with the brioche mixture, pressing it in lightly, and transfer to the oven tray. Grill or bake for 3 minutes.

To serve, put 2 large spoonfuls of barley mixture on each plate. Top with some slices of pork and 2 filled prawns. Arrange a little fried beetroot on the very top, and drizzle chive sauce over the prawns and around the plate.

Insalata di polpo con baccalà mantecato – Avocado and octopus salad with salted-cod paste

For a few years in the late 1980s and early 1990s, avocado suffered from an image problem, with far too many ordinary chicken-and-avocado pastas available around town. But it's a great fruit and worthy of an upmarket menu. In this dish it gets to share a plate with some classic Italian flavours and there's a bit of Spanish influence, too, from my brother-in-law, Chris Rodriguez. ❧ *Serves 4*

2 waxy potatoes (preferably Spunta), peeled and finely diced

4 cloves garlic, peeled

2 sprigs rosemary

sea salt and freshly ground black pepper

500 ml olive oil

20 cherry tomatoes

2 avocadoes

300 g pickled octopus, diced

300 g baccalà mantecato (see page 29)

CELERY OIL

leaves from 1 bunch celery

250 ml olive oil

Preheat the oven to 120ºC. Spread the potato in an ovenproof dish with 2 cloves of garlic, 1 sprig of rosemary and a little salt and pepper. Pour in enough olive oil to just cover. Spread the cherry tomatoes in another ovenproof dish and pour in enough olive oil to just cover. Bake the potato for 40 minutes and the tomatoes for 15 minutes, until both are tender. Allow to cool.

To make the celery oil, blanch the celery leaves in boiling water for 10 seconds, refresh in cold water, drain and squeeze out any excess water. Transfer to a food processor and blend with the olive oil until smooth. Refrigerate overnight to let the colour and flavour infuse, then strain through muslin. Keep refrigerated until ready to serve.

To make the gazpacho (ingredients opposite), put the tomato, cucumber, capsicum, onion, garlic, paprika and bread in a food processor and blend until smooth. Transfer to a bowl and mix in the vinegar, water and olive oil. Add Tabasco sauce to taste, adjust the seasoning and strain through a fine sieve. Refrigerate.

GAZPACHO

400 g ripe Roma tomatoes, chopped

100 g continental cucumber, peeled, chopped and seeded

50 g red capsicum, seeded and chopped

½ small red onion, chopped

1 clove garlic, peeled

pinch of paprika

50 g white bread, crusts removed

50 ml sherry vinegar

250 ml cold water

50 ml extra-virgin olive oil

Tabasco sauce

sea salt and freshly ground black pepper

Dice the avocadoes and fold through the pickled octopus. Taste and adjust the seasoning. To serve, put some avocado mixture on each plate and shape into a ring 8 cm in diameter and 4 cm high. Using 2 dessertspoons, form a quenelle (an oval-shaped ball) with the *baccalà* and put it on top of the avocado. Sprinkle some potato around and arrange 5 cherry tomatoes neatly among the potatoes. To finish, drizzle celery oil and gazpacho around the plate.

Gli Amici

Top-quality raw produce and ingredients are unarguably essential to creating great dishes. But without producers committed to achieving a superior standard there is nothing; they are vital members of the restaurant team. Grossi Florentino is fortunate in being surrounded by many fine producers in Melbourne and to have the resources to draw on those beyond. Most become *amici*, or friends, over time, and the results are on the table. Here are just a few of those *amici*.

Con Andronis from **Clamms Fast Fish** is Guy Grossi's wake-up call. Six days a week Con is on the phone to Guy at 6.30 a.m., advising what fish and seafood are available. Con and his partner, George Kaparos, are wholesalers with a retail outlet in St Kilda who supply about 350 restaurants with produce flown in from around the country. They are always on the lookout for new products and know that Guy will often take something different in addition to his standard order, such as coral trout, or a particularly fine bit of yellowfin tuna. Guy has dealt with Con and George for about 17 of the 25 years they've been in business. 'With fish, you have to pay

because quality and reliability are so important. I've had other suppliers but I always come back to Clamms,' Guy says.

For special or high-quality dry goods and condiments, Guy heads to **Simon Johnson**'s Fitzroy warehouse. Whether it's tuna in oil, organic lentils, melt-in-the-mouth chocolate, coffee, anchovies or dry pasta, Simon tracks down the very best and imports it from the source. In many instances this is a small, artisan-driven and, where possible, organic producer, such as the Italian Colonna oil produced by Princess Marina Colonna and featured on each table in the Restaurant.

Simon and Roger Ongarato's shop on Fitzroy's Brunswick Street cafe strip, **Largo Butchers**, is a treasure trove of genuine *casalinga* salami, prosciutto, pancetta and *cotechino*, all produced to recipes and procedures followed for six generations. 'Everything is dried naturally and it makes a world of difference,' says Guy. The Ongaratos grow all their own beef at Romsey, north of Melbourne, where the cattle are 100 per cent grass-fed, there are no growth stimulants and it's all very

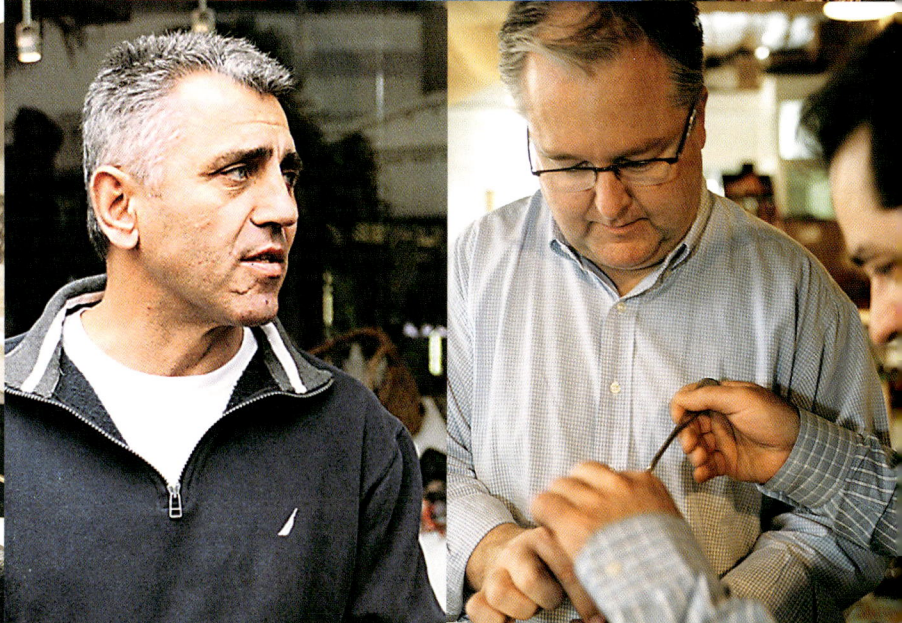

THIS PAGE, TOP
Roger Ongarato at
Largo Butchers.

OPPOSITE
Angelo Butera
(bending) of Fruit
Addiction with Joe Ruffo
(obscured) and Guy at
Tripod Farmers.

hands-on. Once culled, the meat is hung for a month. Guy likes to cook *capretto* (kid) from Largo Butchers, and they are also his source of milk-fed veal and lamb.

Frank Candeloro was the first 'fancy lettuce' grower in Australia, using seeds he brought with him from Sicily. Now his daughter, Carmel, and son-in-law, Joe Ruffo, produce Australia's best baby spinach at Tripod Farmers at Bacchus Marsh, west of Melbourne. Their spinach is bought by a select clientele around the country, and also exported to Asia – as are their lettuces (including butter, cos, coral and mignonette) and wild rocket. The greens are hand-picked by a team of about forty, overseen by Carmel, and this labour-intensive effort produces a superior product. Also essential is the 'cold chain' that preserves the produce, from the coolroom to cool-storage trucks. Planted weekly and harvested daily, the various salad vegetables are transported to Footscray Market, where Angelo Butera of Fruit Addiction selects them for Grossi Florentino.

Quaglia arrosto con couscous –
Thyme-roasted quail with couscous
and sheep's-milk yoghurt

Couscous is commonly used in Sicily, where the Arab influence is still apparent in the culture and architecture. The Arabs ruled Sicily after the Ancient Greeks and brought many new foods with them. They also taught the Sicilians new techniques, such as making sorbets (*gelato*). Large-grain couscous is available from specialist food stores. ∾ *Serves 4*

4 cloves garlic, chopped

½ small chilli, seeded and chopped

½ cup freshly chopped flat-leaf parsley

1 cup freshly chopped thyme

olive oil

sea salt and freshly ground black pepper

4 large quails

1 large onion, cut in half

1 large carrot, cut in half

1 stalk celery, cut in half

4 handfuls mixed herbs (chervil, coriander, parsley and dill), picked into sprigs

200 g large-grain couscous

750 ml chicken stock (see page 215)

4 teaspoons butter

100 ml sheep's milk yoghurt (preferably Meredith)

4 teaspoons verjuice

4 quail eggs

In a ceramic or glass dish, combine half the garlic with the chilli, parsley, thyme, a little olive oil and salt and pepper to taste. Using a large knife or cleaver, chop the quails in half across the centre so that you are left with one half containing the breast and the other containing the legs. Add the breasts to the marinade and marinate for at least 30 minutes.

Preheat the oven to 200°C. Roughly chop one half of the onion, carrot and celery, and finely dice the other. Scatter the roughly chopped onion, carrot and celery in a shallow roasting tray and put the quail legs on top. Season with salt and pepper and roast for about 10 minutes. Remove from the oven and allow to cool a little, then pull the meat from the bones and set the meat aside. Reduce the oven temperature to 180°C.

Heat a little olive oil in a pan and fry the finely chopped vegetables, the remaining garlic and the mixed herbs until soft. Add the couscous and toss well before stirring in a small amount of stock. When it has been absorbed, add a little more. Continue to add small amounts of stock until the couscous is cooked but still a little al dente – this will take about 20 minutes (you may not need to use all of the stock). Add the meat from the quail legs and stir in the butter, letting it melt through the mixture.

Combine the yoghurt and verjuice and season to taste with salt and pepper. Heat a little olive oil in a frying pan until hot and add the quail breasts. Seal each side, then transfer to the oven for 3 minutes. Allow to cool a little, then remove the breasts from the carcass. Fry the quail eggs in a little olive oil for 1–2 minutes over a low heat, until the whites are cooked but the yolks are still runny. To serve, spoon some couscous onto each plate and put a quail breast on top, then an egg. Drizzle over some yoghurt dressing and top with a neat mixture of herbs. If you wish, serve *agresto* (see page 215) alongside.

Piccione arrosto al vin santo – Oven-roasted pigeon with sweet wine sauce

These plump game birds are typical of the north of Italy. I buy mine from Glenloth Game, as they are consistent in flavour and texture. *Cotechino*, a rich pork sausage traditional to northern Italy, adds a luxurious texture. ❧ *Vin santo* ('saintly wine') is a Tuscan dessert wine, usually sweet but sometimes dry and sherry-like, made from semidried grapes. ❧ *Serves 4*

1 cotechino sausage

6 bay leaves

1 onion, roughly chopped

1 carrot, roughly chopped

1 stalk celery, roughly chopped

4 rosemary branches

4 cloves garlic

4 × 350 g pigeons

olive oil

sea salt and freshly ground black pepper

1 star anise, crushed

4 juniper berries, crushed

4 thin slices of truffle (optional)

Put the *cotechino* and 2 bay leaves in a pot and cover with water. Bring to the boil, then reduce the heat and gently simmer for 1 hour, topping up the water if necessary.

Meanwhile, preheat the oven to 200°C. Scatter the vegetables and rosemary in a roasting tray. Put 1 clove of garlic and 1 bay leaf inside each pigeon. Heat a little olive oil in a frying pan and sear each bird until it is light gold in colour. Transfer the birds to the roasting tray and season with salt, pepper, star anise and juniper. Bake for 15 minutes. Using a boning knife, carefully remove the meat from the carcasses, keeping the 2 halves intact. Set aside and keep warm.

To make the sauce (ingredients opposite), sauté the vegetables in a little olive oil until soft. Deglaze with the vin santo, then add the chicken stock and reduce by half over a moderate heat. Strain through a fine sieve and reduce again until you are left with about 1 cup of sauce.

To make the peas and pancetta (ingredients opposite), blanch the peas in boiling water for 1 minute, then run under cold water until cool. Heat a little olive oil in a pot and sauté the onion, garlic and pancetta for 2–3 minutes.

VIN SANTO SAUCE

½ small onion, roughly chopped

½ carrot, roughly chopped

½ stalk celery, roughly chopped

olive oil

750 ml vin santo *or* other sweet wine

1 litre chicken stock (see page 215)

PEAS AND PANCETTA

1 kg fresh peas, podded

olive oil

1 onion, diced

2 cloves garlic, finely chopped

100 g pancetta, diced

4 mint leaves, chopped

250 ml chicken stock (see page 215)

sea salt and freshly ground black pepper

Add the peas, mint and stock and cook for 10 minutes over a moderate heat. Season to taste with salt and pepper.

Allow the *cotechino* to cool a little, then cut into 5 mm slices. To serve, spoon some peas into the centre of each plate and top with a slice of *cotechino*. Arrange 2 pigeon halves on the *cotechino* and pour a little sauce over the top and around the plate. Finish off with a thin slice of truffle, if using.

Abbacchio alla romana – Wet roast of suckling lamb with herbs, breadcrumbs and Parmigiano-Reggiano

This is a long-time family favourite and one of the Florentino's most popular dishes. Part of the joy of making it is massaging the pieces of lamb with your fingertips. I source lamb from the Barossa Valley in South Australia or Mt Emu in Victoria. It is most important that your meat is young – less than three months is preferable. It will be succulent and tender, with a delicate flavour. I look for plump, well-fed lambs that have a decent coat of fat and a full weight of 5–8 kg. ∿ *Serves 4*

2.5 kg suckling lamb pieces (leg and loin)

1 small onion, finely chopped

2 tomatoes, chopped

½ cup finely chopped sage

leaves from 3 sprigs rosemary, finely chopped

2 bay leaves

1 cup freshly chopped flat-leaf parsley

3 cloves garlic, finely chopped

1 chilli, seeded and finely chopped

500 ml white wine

sea salt and freshly ground black pepper

200 ml olive oil

2 litres chicken stock (see page 215)

100 g breadcrumbs

150 g freshly grated Parmigiano-Reggiano

Preheat the oven to 180°C. Put the lamb pieces in a deep roasting tray and add the onion, tomato, herbs, garlic, chilli and white wine. Season with salt and pepper and drizzle with the olive oil. With your fingertips, massage the oil into each piece of lamb. Pour in the stock and sprinkle with the breadcrumbs and Parmigiano-Reggiano. Bake for 45–50 minutes (or less for very young lamb), until the meat is very tender and has a golden-brown crust. Serve with roasted potatoes or baked artichokes.

Sella di cervo – Saddle of venison with cassoulet of beans

Venison is a great introduction to game, as its flavour is subtle. It is a lean meat, which is why a little cooking is better than a lot, especially for primary cuts like the saddle. Of course, some of the secondary cuts make a great casserole. I prefer to use Southern Gold potatoes here as they are waxy and yellow and hold together well in the bean cassoulet. Cannellini beans are a pantry staple in the restaurant and at home. They are easy to cook and can be turned into a heart-warming soup or a side dish. ∽ *Serves 4*

8 × 150 g venison chops

20 g butter

100 g dandelion chicory leaves

sea salt and freshly ground black pepper

MARINADE FOR VENISON

1 teaspoon crushed juniper berries

3 cloves garlic, sliced

2 sprigs rosemary, broken into pieces

sea salt and freshly ground black pepper

30 ml olive oil

BEAN CASSOULET

20 ml olive oil

1 clove garlic, chopped

1 small onion, finely diced

1 carrot, finely diced

1 stalk celery, finely diced

50 g speck, finely diced

2 × 50 g pork sausages

200 g dried cannellini beans, soaked overnight

1 litre chicken stock (see page 215)

2 medium waxy potatoes (preferably Southern Gold), finely diced

sea salt and freshly ground black pepper

Trim the venison chops of any excess fat. To make the marinade, mix all the ingredients in a glass or ceramic dish. Add the chops, turning to coat with the marinade. Refrigerate for 2 hours.

To make the cassoulet, heat the olive oil in a pot and add the garlic. Sauté briefly but do not allow to colour. Add the onion and sauté for a few minutes, then add the carrot, celery and speck and cook for a further 5 minutes or until they start to soften. Add the sausages, cannellini beans, sautéed vegetables and speck. Fry for a couple of minutes, then pour in the stock and simmer for 10 minutes. Add the potato and cook gently on a medium–low heat for 30 minutes until the beans are just soft. Lift out the sausages, slice roughly and return to the pot. Season to taste with salt and pepper. The cassoulet should be a little runny – the liquid from it will flavour the finished dish beautifully.

Preheat the oven to 180°C. Seal the chops in an ovenproof frying pan on both sides until golden brown, then put in the oven for about 5 minutes, or longer if you like them cooked more. Meanwhile, melt the butter in a frying pan and sauté the chicory leaves with some salt and pepper until just wilted.

To serve, put a spoonful of the cassoulet in the middle of each plate. Arrange 2 venison chops on the cassoulet and drape some chicory leaves over.

La Cucina

The kitchen is Grossi Florentino's engine room, the bustling nucleus that literally feeds the whole operation. Once the domain of Salvatore and Costa, the Florentino's most famous chefs of the past, *la cucina* is now the charged environment in which Guy Grossi creates, finesses and experiments to a demanding timetable. 'It is not a calm environment,' he says with understatement.

First to arrive at 5 a.m. is the pastry chef, let in by the cleaners who are already at work and putting out the sidewalk furniture. Doughs are prepared, then the pastries, bread and other breakfast needs of the Cellar Bar, which opens at 7.30. The storeman and Cellar Bar cook arrive at seven, and by nine the Grill and Restaurant cooks are on deck. Produce starts to arrive and the kitchen gets very busy checking and storing it, or sending it downstairs to the Grill. Pots are on the stove as the daily preparation of stocks and sauces begins, and the ovens are reclaimed from the pastry chef (who knocks off around 4 p.m.).

When the fish and seafood arrive, no one wants the job of scrubbing the mussels (Guy insists that no debris is left on) or cleaning the calamari. Meanwhile, loads of parsley has to be chopped and at least four boxes of spinach plucked, washed and blanched, which alone can take two hours. The fight is always against time: by 11.45 a.m. the floors must be swept and the benches wiped clean for lunchtime service. By now Guy has worked his way through three coffees and the first orders are in.

Once lunch is over, the benches are wiped clean again and preparation for the evening continues, including changes to the menu specials. 'This can go on until 5.30 p.m. – we never know,' says Guy. He controls all the orders and helps chef Chris Rodriguez serve the main courses, checking every dish before it goes out. The kitchen closes between 11 p.m. and midnight, when there is another clean-up. Last out is the dessert chef, followed by the dishwashers at about 1 a.m.

While these days tension in the kitchen is over time and space, it has always been a heated environment, where tensions boiled and personalities clashed. In the restaurant's early days, Rinaldo

Massoni's fondness for a flutter was as nothing compared to that of his celebrated chef, the tall, handsome Salvatore.

A former sweet cook to Italy's King Victor Emmanuel, Salvatore was brought to Australia by Adelaide's South Australia Hotel with his friend and fellow chef Ernesto Molina. He was renowned for creating elaborate decorations from butter, sugar and icing, and Lolita Massoni (Leon's late sister) recalled him making her birthday cakes, and flowers of spun sugar to put at each place setting for her girlfriends. He created the signature dessert Crêpes Florentino – a pastry cream filling of his own secret nuts-and-nougat concoction, and a top caramelised with a red-hot poker – and made Australia's first cassata. But he was a compulsive gambler who lost most of his considerable wage at the races or cards, which he played every night until the wee hours. When he lost, which was usual, his cooking was superb; when he won, it wasn't, according to Allan Wynn in *The Fortunes of Samuel Wynn*.

Salvatore frequently quarrelled with Rinaldo, whom he adored, and resigned often. But he never lowered his standards, and to him a spoilt sauce was a personal outrage. He once threw his gold watch – a gift from the king of Italy – into a bowl of sauce gone wrong. On another occasion, in a rage at a losing racehorse, he demolished, with one swipe of a meat axe, four days of painstaking work on an ice sculpture of a Gothic cathedral. The most famous Salvatore story, however, is of when he went missing and was eventually discovered flat out and frozen in the cold-storage room, where a kitchenhand had unwittingly imprisoned him. Revived by having Cognac rubbed on his hands and face and poured down his throat, he reached for his biggest carving knife and sharpened it meaningfully. No one spoke; everyone departed.

Costa, a Greek trained in both French and Italian cuisine, was the antithesis of the flamboyant, temperamental Salvatore: shy and reserved and disliking publicity. When George Tsindos acquired sole ownership, he opted for a French chef and an Italian chef working a half-day each, to give the kitchen more flexibility. Costa was the French chef, Tony Adami the Italian and they were with George for twenty years, during much of which time Costa was the only Greek at the all-Italian Florentino – except for the owner, who in any case spoke perfect Italian.

Budini al rabarbaro – Rhubarb and tapioca puddings with prosecco zabaglione

These lovely baked puddings make you feel like a kid again. Whenever anybody says 'zabaglione' I picture my mother at breakfast time, beating eggs with a fork to make the light, frothy mixture of yolks, sugar and liqueur (usually marsala). What a way to start the day! ∿ *Serves 4*

2 tablespoons pearl tapioca

250 ml milk

1 stalk rhubarb, peeled and cut into 1 cm pieces

20 g caster sugar

2 tablespoons melted butter

1 cup soft breadcrumbs

1 cup raisins

150 g brown sugar

1 tablespoon finely chopped preserved ginger (optional)

1 teaspoon bicarbonate of soda

4 clementines (see page 212), cut into segments

PROSECCO ZABAGLIONE

3 egg yolks

25 g caster sugar

100 ml white wine

150 ml prosecco *or* other light dry white wine

Soak the tapioca in the milk overnight. Next day, grease 4 dariole moulds and preheat the oven to 160°C. Put the rhubarb in a small pot with the sugar and a little water. Cook over a low heat until darkened to a caramel colour.

Stir the melted butter into the breadcrumbs, then add the raisins, brown sugar, ginger (if using) and bicarbonate of soda. Add the soaked tapioca and mix well. The mixture should have the consistency of porridge; if it is not runny enough, add a little more milk. Put a little rhubarb in each dariole mould and fill with tapioca mixture. Cover each mould with foil and transfer to a baking tray. Pour in water until it reaches two-thirds the way up the moulds. Bake for 1½ hours or until the puddings spring back when touched. Remove from the oven and allow to cool.

To make the *zabaglione*, put the yolks, sugar, wine and prosecco in a large bowl. Whisk over a pan of simmering water on a medium–low heat, turning the bowl and whisking continuously, until the *zabaglione* is light and fluffy.

Turn the warm puddings out on medium-sized plates and arrange some clementine segments around. Spoon some *zabaglione* around the plates and drizzle a little over the puddings. Serve with fresh berry coulis, if desired.

Panna cotta al caffe – Coffee-flavoured cream with tuile biscuits, Armagnac custard and vin santo jelly

Panna cotta originated in Piemonte and has found its way onto menus worldwide due to its versatility and relative simplicity. You can let your imagination go wild with flavours, using anything from rosewater to rum. The challenge is to make the necessary adjustments so your *panna cotta* will set but not turn into a hard, rubbery 'tennis ball'. ~ *Serves 8*

4 gelatine leaves

1 litre cream

200 ml strong espresso coffee

150 g caster sugar

few drops of vincotto (optional)

VIN SANTO JELLY

3 gelatine leaves

225 ml vin santo

75 ml sugar syrup (see page 218)

TUILES

150 g softened butter

300 g icing sugar

7 egg whites

175 g flour

1 teaspoon vanilla extract

icing sugar

ARMAGNAC CUSTARD

250 ml milk

250 ml cream

5 egg yolks

30 g cornflour

110 g caster sugar

2 teaspoons Armagnac *or* brandy

Soak the gelatine leaves in cold water for a few minutes, then squeeze out any excess moisture. In a small saucepan, heat half the cream with the coffee and sugar. When almost at boiling point, remove from the heat and mix in the gelatine. Cool. Whip the remaining cream to soft peaks and fold into the coffee mixture. Pour into 8 dariole moulds and chill for 3 hours, or until set.

To make the *vin santo* jelly, soak the gelatine leaves in cold water as above. Heat the *vin santo* in a small pot with the sugar syrup. When the mixture is near boiling point, whisk in the gelatine. Pour into a tray and chill.

To make the tuiles, preheat the oven to 160ºC and grease a baking tray with butter or spray. Mix the butter and icing sugar to a paste. Whisk the egg whites until soft peaks form, then gently fold into the butter mixture. Sift the flour over and lightly fold in. Stir in the vanilla and rest for 5 minutes. Spoon tablespoons of tuile batter onto the tray – you need to make 16 biscuits. Bake for 7–8 minutes or until golden around the edges. Just before they have fully cooled, roll each tuile around the handle of a wooden spoon. If they have already hardened, reheat briefly in the oven and try again. Leave to cool on a wire rack.

To make the custard, boil the milk and cream together in a saucepan. Whisk the egg yolks, cornflour and sugar in a bowl. Whisk in a little of the boiling milk/cream, then gradually add the rest. Return to the saucepan and cook for 3 minutes over a medium heat. Do not overcook. Transfer to a clean bowl, cover with plastic wrap and chill. Whisk the Armagnac into the cold custard until smooth (adding a little extra Armagnac, if desired) and transfer to a piping bag. Pipe into the tuiles and dust with icing sugar.

Using a potato masher, mash the jelly until it breaks into small pieces. Unmould each *panna cotta* onto a plate and put 2 tuiles and a little *vin santo* jelly next to it. Add a few drops of *vincotto*, if desired.

Tartine di pomodoro – Sweet tomato tarts

Tomato is a fruit, so why not use it in a dessert? Its natural sweetness is intensified by cooking. Here I cook the tomatoes with sugar just as I would plums. The fruit is surprisingly resilient and holds up well. The yoghurt provides a refreshing contrast to the spices. ∿ *Serves 4*

4 large Roma tomatoes, cored

500 ml sugar syrup (see page 218)

2 star anise

1 cinnamon stick

1 clove

½ teaspoon vanilla extract

1 tablespoon raspberry coulis *or* raspberry jam

250 g sheep's milk yoghurt (preferably Meredith)

1 tablespoon icing sugar

250 ml cream

leaves from 8 sprigs mint, washed

PASTRY

125 g self-raising flour

125 g plain flour

50 g caster sugar

250 g unsalted butter, at room temperature

hot water

To make the pastry, sift the flours together into a bowl and add the sugar. Work the butter into the flour until the mixture resembles breadcrumbs. Add a little hot water and work to a paste. Wrap in plastic wrap and refrigerate for at least 1 hour before use. Preheat the oven to 180°C. Gently roll out the pastry on a floured surface and press into 4 individual tart cases 8 cm in diameter. Bake for 10–15 minutes or until golden brown. Allow to cool.

Meanwhile, blanch the tomatoes in boiling water for 1 minute and refresh in iced water. Peel the skin off, cut the tomatoes in half and remove the seeds. Bring the sugar syrup, spices, vanilla and raspberry coulis to the boil in a saucepan. Simmer and reduce for 5 minutes. Add the tomatoes and continue to simmer for 10 minutes until they are just tender. Using a slotted spoon, transfer the tomatoes to a tray, leaving all the juices in the pot. Continue to reduce the juices until they reach a thick, syrupy consistency. Allow to cool.

Combine the yoghurt and icing sugar. Whip the cream until soft peaks form, then fold into the yoghurt. Pat the mint leaves dry and bruise gently in a mortar and pestle. Put each tart case on a serving plate and spoon in some yoghurt mixture. Arrange 2 cooled tomato halves on top and drizzle with syrup. Garnish with a few bruised mint leaves and serve with vanilla ice-cream.

Dolce misto di cioccolata Valrhona – Valrhona Grands Crus chocolate dessert

Valrhona is considered one of the absolute best producers of chocolate in the world. I designed this elegant dessert to highlight some of their individual plantation chocolate varieties, each of which has a unique character. The plantations are in Madagascar, the Caribbean and South America, and the flavour of the beans reflects the earth of their origin. The various chocolates also contain slightly different amounts of cocoa, which affects their flavour. ∿ *Serves 4*

4 scoops Valrhona chocolate ice-cream
(see page 205)

GANACHE

185 ml heavy cream

115 g Valrhona 'Guanaja' chocolate,
finely chopped

CHOCOLATE CAKES

100 g Valrhona 'Guanaja' chocolate, chopped

60 g softened unsalted butter

3 large eggs, separated

30 g flour

20 g almond meal

50 g caster sugar

icing sugar

To make the ganache, heat the cream to just below boiling point and pour it over the chocolate. When the chocolate begins to melt, stir gently to combine. Pour into a small, flat, rectangular dish and refrigerate until set. Cut the ganache into 3 cm squares and chill until needed.

To make the cakes, preheat the oven to 160°C. Melt the chocolate in a double boiler, gently stir in the butter and remove from the heat. Rest for 5 minutes, then whisk in the egg yolks one at a time. Sift the flour and almond meal and fold into the chocolate mixture. Beat the egg whites to form soft peaks, then fold into the batter one-third at a time. Grease 4 small moulds and fill them three-quarters full with the batter. Add a piece of chocolate ganache and fill with batter. Bake for 20 minutes or until the tops of the cakes are firm.

Meanwhile, make the choc-malt shakes. Put the milk, cream and malt extract in a saucepan over a medium heat and stir until almost boiling. Remove from the heat and pour over the chocolate. Allow to rest for a minute, then use a hand-held blender to combine to a milk-shake consistency. If the mixture is too thick, add a little extra milk. Cool and transfer to 4 shot glasses.

CHOC-MALT SHAKES

100 ml milk

300 ml cream

1 tablespoon malt extract

75 g Valrhona 'Caraïbe' chocolate, chopped

Serve the dessert on oval-shaped plates. Turn out the warm chocolate puddings and dust with icing sugar. Put one in the middle of each plate, with a scoop of chocolate ice-cream on one side and a glass of choc-malt shake on the other.

Gelati della casa – Homemade ice-creams

Gelato literally means 'frozen'. The Sicilians were given the concept by the Arabs in the eleventh century and have been perfecting it ever since. *Gelato* – whether water-based or milk-based – is quite simple to make, but you do need an ice-cream churn or machine. ❧ *Makes approximately 1 litre of each ice-cream*

CARAMEL ICE-CREAM

450 ml milk

450 ml cream

seeds from 1 vanilla bean

10 egg yolks

230 g caster sugar

300 g Callebaut caramel chocolate

VALRHONA CHOCOLATE ICE-CREAM

500 ml milk

300 ml water

300 g caster sugar

80 ml liquid glucose

60 g cocoa

250 g Valrhona 'Manjari' chocolate

LEMON GELATO

500 ml lemon juice

500 ml sugar syrup (see page 218)

STRAWBERRY GELATO

500 ml strawberry purée

500 ml sugar syrup (see page 218)

20 ml lemon juice

To make the caramel ice-cream, bring the milk and cream to the boil with the vanilla seeds. Combine the egg yolks and sugar in a large bowl and mix in a little of the boiling milk/cream. Slowly add the rest of the milk/cream, stirring. Return to the pot and cook over a medium heat for 10–15 minutes, stirring constantly, until the mixture coats the back of a spoon. Chop the chocolate and put it in a large bowl. Pour over the custard mixture and whisk until there are no lumps. Allow to cool. Churn in an ice-cream machine to a 'soft serve' consistency, then transfer to a container and freeze until required.

To make the chocolate ice-cream, combine all the ingredients except the chocolate and bring to the boil over a high heat. Chop the chocolate and put it in a large bowl. Pour over the boiling mixture and mix well until there are no lumps. Allow to cool completely. Churn in an ice-cream machine to a 'soft serve' consistency, then transfer to a container and freeze until required.

To make the lemon gelato and strawberry gelato, combine the respective ingredients and churn (separately) in an ice-cream machine to a 'soft serve' consistency. Transfer to a container and freeze until required.

Serve a scoop of each ice-cream, garnished appropriately – for example, shards of toffee, a chocolate stick or chocolate curls, a slice or two of strawberry, and candied lemon zest.

Soffiato di cioccolato – Chocolate soufflé

A soufflé has a festive feel, adding a sense of occasion and, sometimes, drama. The Florentino chocolate soufflé is one of those dishes we would not even attempt to remove from our menu – there would be a revolution! After all these years it still outsells every other dessert. It is a dish of French origin, of course, but has a place on Grossi Florentino's menu as a testament to Melbourne's cultural history and a reminder of a time when a menu wasn't 'Italian' or 'French' but 'Continental'. We serve it with a scoop of malt ice-cream drowned in espresso coffee. ∾ *Serves 12*

65 g cocoa

100 g cornflour

500 ml milk

unsalted butter

caster sugar

50 ml brandy

16 egg whites

icing sugar

Combine the cocoa, cornflour and half the milk and whisk until there are no lumps. Put the remaining milk in a pot and bring to the boil. Remove from the heat and pour gradually into the cocoa mixture, stirring. Mix well, then return the mixture to the pot and whisk over a medium heat for 3–4 minutes until very thick and smooth. Set aside to cool.

Preheat the oven to 200°C. Grease 12 soufflé dishes (9 cm in diameter) with butter and sprinkle with caster sugar. Whisk the egg whites until they form stiff peaks, gradually adding 225 g caster sugar as you whisk.

Transfer the cooled chocolate mixture to a large bowl. Blend in the brandy, then whisk in one-third of the egg whites, incorporating well. Gently fold in the remaining egg whites and thoroughly incorporate. Gently transfer to the prepared moulds and bake for 7–10 minutes. Dust with a generous amount of icing sugar and serve immediately.

La Cucina Italiana

The Italian *cucina* ('style of cooking') is regional, affected by an area's origins, soil and historical influences. Within a region, the *cucina* varies from town to town and even from family to family. It is not fixed, and when transported far from its origins will always grow and develop. Melbourne is no exception: the great Italian *cucina* has found a home here and been welcomed with open arms. Italian cooks have, in turn, explored the local culture and it has left its influence. Thus the food from Grossi Florentino's kitchen has a Melbourne stamp on it.nd best-known restaurant business.

For me, the relentless pursuit of quality is an obsession. Quality begins with the raw product, but beyond that I believe it is important not to be bound by rigid rules, because cooking must be expressive and personal. Tradition is essential, giving a foundation on which to build, but the rest must flow without restriction and your environment becomes what you make it.

Chris Rodriguez and I discuss food at the slightest provocation. Beginning with something one of us has seen, we bounce around ideas that are later assimilated into an existing recipe or become a new dish. As Chris and I spend nearly all of our work and social time together, this process occurs anywhere. Sometimes an idea will blossom in a flash; at other times we will change it a hundred times and have a spat over it.

The family is, of course, an endless source of inspiration. Whether it be a simple meal Melissa cooks for me and our children, Carlo and Loredana, or a Sunday visit to Chris's parents for his mum's paella, or a single ingredient or technique, once you get involved with food your mind never really switches off.

In the end Chris's and my food is like us: rooted in tradition but modified by our environment – Melbourne food, Italian style. Here are our thoughts on the fundamentals, followed by some recipes for essential sauces, stocks and pastry from Grossi Florentino's own *cucina*.

PASTA There are many opinions on *pasta fatta in casa* (homemade pasta) versus *pasta secca* (dry pasta). The fact is that they are two different products, each with its own place and each found in varying degrees of quality. We make much of our own pasta, using golden, hard durum-wheat flour. It makes fantastic pasta that can be dried or used fresh. We also buy commercially produced pasta; I like the Martelli brand, as it is a high-quality product.

Pasta has a wonderful flavour that is best appreciated by cooking it properly in plenty of boiling salted water and eating it without sauce. Use it straight away and never refresh it under cold running water, as this washes the pasta and will dilute its floury flavour.

'Butta la pasta,' rings through the household when dinner is close. It means 'throw the pasta' into the water, and also that if you are late to the table you'll have only yourself

to blame if the pasta is overcooked. Having said that, there are many degrees of *cottura* (cooking) and some people prefer pasta cooked longer than the al dente stage. When I was young I preferred my pasta *al filo di fero* ('like steel wire'), but these days I settle for al dente.

CHOP V. CRUSH Whether you chop or crush an ingredient has an effect upon its properties, and this is very important when dealing with pungent foods such as garlic and onions. For example, garlic for pesto should be crushed in a mortar and pestle (a must-have item in the kitchen), but if garlic is required for *soffritto* (see page 30), it needs to be chopped so its juices are not lost and the garlic is not bruised.

GREMOLATA *Gremolata* is a *battuto* (literally meaning 'beaten') of parsley, lemon rind and garlic chopped together and used to flavour osso buco and other casserole dishes. When baking whole fish I like to put a little *gremolata* inside the fish and drizzle it with olive oil and lemon juice. Mint, garlic, sage and parsley make up the very Roman *battuto* used to dress *carciofi* (artichokes) prior to cooking them in oil.

CHEESE Chris and I love cheese, and we take on the responsibility of choosing for the menu just so we can try different varieties! A piece of cheese is like a storybook, telling you about the place it came from. Matching cheese with wine and accompaniments is a lot of fun, too.

Parmigiano One of the most common ingredients in our kitchen. We use both Grana Padano and Reggiano for grating as seasoning, but Reggiano is our preferred table cheese. Good-quality aged Parmigiano has a sharp palate with a salty taste. Always buy a whole piece and grate it as required, as it retains its flavour this way.

Gorgonzola I prefer *gorgonzola piccante* to *gorgonzola dolce latte* (sweet milk gorgonzola). The bite on the tongue combined with the piquancy of the cultures is what I enjoy most. *Dolce latte* has a more mellow taste.

Mozzarella Buffalo milk is traditionally used to make this bright white cheese. Its subtle flavours make it versatile and great in cooking, but it is at its best simply served with an excellent olive oil. Bocconcini (literally 'little mouthfuls') are a popular variation of mozzarella.

Pecorino Pecorino is similar to Parmigiano-Reggiano in appearance, but the taste is totally different, as it is made from sheep's rather than cow's milk. Pecorino is grated onto many pasta dishes and salads.

FLOUR AND SPELT *Farina* (flour) plays an enormous part in our kitchen. There are many types, with various purposes. I have found *farro*, a type of spelt, to be very exciting. Spelt is an ancient variety of wheat, native to southern Europe, which is starting to become popular again. We use local spelt flour, which is sensational in our bread. It adds density and an old-fashioned, homemade flavour. As a grain, spelt can be used just like rice to make a great risotto-style dish. I also love it in soup, called *minestra di farro*.

GARLIC AND ONION   Garlic (*aglio*) and onion (*cipolla*) are the king and queen of the Italian kitchen. In many of this book's recipes, they are sweated together in olive oil before any other ingredient is added; this base is a vital part of the dish. Take time to cook the onions and garlic gently until they are soft, when the sugars will be released from the onions and you will be rewarded with a delicious flavour. In any recipe, use only fresh garlic cloves and prepare only what you require. If you find onion a little overpowering, try substituting golden shallots, which give a sweeter flavour.

HERBS   Our kitchen depends on many herbs, most of them common herbs that have been grown for centuries in Europe. I can't imagine roasting meats without them. There is a flavour that cannot be denied about garden-grown produce. Depth of flavour comes from balance in the use of ingredients, and herbs are no exception. Handled with sensitivity, they will elevate your *cucina*.

Rosemary   Native to the Mediterranean coast (and the front lawn!), rosemary is immediately associated with Italian food. The oil in the leaves flavours foods well.

Sage   Its name coming from *salvere*, the Latin for 'to save' or 'to heal', sage has always been connected to good health. Its flavour is strong and needs a suitable partner, for example, calf's liver.

Parsley   I prefer the flat-leaf variety, as it has a slightly stronger and more defined taste. We use enormous amounts. Remember to include the stalks in stocks, sauces and *mirepoix*, as they impart an enormous amount of flavour.

Basil   A wonderful herb that can be eaten straight from the garden, the basil plant is extremely variable. The quality and strength of the taste depends on the oils in the leaves. Basil should be picked in the morning, when its flavour is strongest; the oils are more concentrated when the plant is cooler. Leaves picked from the same plant in full sun later in the day will not have as strong a flavour. If you are using basil in a cooked dish, it is best added towards the end of the cooking process, so that the flavour and aroma are not lost.

Oregano   Once you have planted oregano and it has established itself, it will be in your garden always. When the shoots grow upwards, cut the long stems, tie the oregano into a bundle with string and hang it upside down to dry. The flavour will intensify and the dried oregano can be kept for months. Oregano is the only herb that works well dried.

MUSHROOMS   Mushroom season is an exciting one in the kitchen. While we are never without dried porcini and wild mushrooms, I love to prepare fresh local morels, slippery jacks and pine mushrooms, just to name a few. When soaking dried mushrooms, always lift the mushrooms from the water rather than straining the water off, as lifting them out leaves the dirt behind in the water. Once the mushrooms have been lifted out gently, drain the liquid into another bowl, leaving the last few centimetres to be discarded. Use this drained liquid in your cooking, as it is full of flavour.

TRUFFLES Fresh truffle is an extravagance I can't do without. We mainly use two varieties of black truffles: the summer black from areas around Umbria and neighbouring northern regions, and the winter black, which is more pungent and has a stronger flavour. Summer blacks are more commonly found and are cheaper than the winter truffles. The white Alba truffle is the prince of them all. The most keenly sought-after and rarest of the truffles, it has the highest intensity of flavour. To store a truffle, put it in a large jar of rice and refrigerate. Eggs can be added to the jar while it is being stored. The flavour of the truffle will permeate the eggs and rice, which can then be used in other dishes once the truffles are finished.

OLIVE OIL Olive oil is our link to ancient history, and is a foundation of our *cucina*. In some cases, different oils alter our cooking style by adding their own personalities and actually driving the course of a dish. I love to work with many oils from diverse areas, each expressing its origin. Olive oil is not just a cooking compound; it is a seasoning, a sauce, a dressing. It is essential, and its world needs to be explored.

CITRUS FRUITS A wedge of **lemon** is always served with fish in the Italian kitchen, but I also like to serve lemon with a simply grilled piece of steak or veal. There is always lemon juice in the kitchen, too, for osso buco, to marinate sardines and to dress salads as a refreshing alternative to vinegar, while grated lemon zest adds a delicate flavour to many savoury meat dishes. Like **oranges**, lemons are also used extensively in desserts, particularly in southern Italy. When choosing lemons, try to buy fruit with a thin skin. Before squeezing a lemon for its juice, roll the fruit on your workbench, pushing down with your palm. This will release the juices and you will be able to extract more liquid. **Clementines** are small oranges and are available in Australia imported from Italy in a heavy syrup. I like to use them in desserts. **Grapefruit** are rarely seen in Italian recipes, but juiced and served on ice with Campari they make a great aperitif. **Cumquats**, like their cousin the clementine, are intensely bitter, and a difficult fruit to use unless you preserve them in sugar. I preserve the cumquats from my father's tree under brandy and sugar, and serve them with duck. I like to use **limes** with seafood, especially prawns.

PULSES The Italian *cucina* has developed over many centuries by utilising foodstuffs at hand. Grains and pulses can be stored for long periods, and are thus available all year round. It is not surprising, then, to see beans dressed with olive oil and vinegar on an antipasto plate during the warmer months, or a hearty soup full of beans that becomes a meal in itself during winter. The pantry should always be well stocked with a selection of these dried goods. The Tuscans are known for their **white bean** recipes, serving them as a purée with meats, with fontina cheese in a soup, or dressed with truffle oil and vinegar as a salad. And *pasta e fagioli* (literally, 'pasta and beans') – there wouldn't be an Italian home kitchen without a version of this soup. I like to add a piece of speck or pancetta to the base of a bean soup, as it gives a wonderful depth and heartiness to the flavour. **Chick peas** and **lentils** (I love lentils from Casteluccio) are featured in northern cooking, along with rice, and are often served with meat or fish, or as the main ingredient in soup. A piece of fresh sausage, such as *cotechino* or *zampone,* marries well with braised lentils.

SALT AND PEPPER Seasoning must be added during the cooking process and not after, as salt and pepper work as natural flavour-enhancers. The best Italian **sea salt** is from Sicily, and comes in two grades. Coarse salt is used for a crust on fish or meat during baking, and is added to water for cooking pasta and vegetables. Fine salt is used at the table, in sauces and to dress raw ingredients when the salt is required to dissolve easily. One of the main uses of salt in the Italian kitchen is for preserving. *Baccalà* is made by salting and then drying cod; the *baccalà* then has to be soaked for days in fresh water before it can be used. Olives and sardines are often preserved in salt. When cooking pasta, the water must be well salted. **Pepper**, whether black or white, is used in generous amounts. Cracked black pepper, freshly ground, is always close at hand by our stoves, but in some dishes I prefer to use white pepper. *Piera*, a sauce my mother makes to serve with boiled meat, is made from white pepper and breadcrumbs, a sensational combination of flavours.

TOMATOES I am always in search of good tomatoes. I remember my father growing them when I was a child, and they were full of flavour and the heat of the sun. Like most fruits, when picked with the stalk still attached, tomatoes will continue to ripen. My father picked tomatoes from his garden before the birds could have their turn, and left them on the window sill to ripen further until my mother used them. Tomatoes were introduced to the southern regions of Italy from Mexico in the 16th century, and it didn't take long for them to become an integral part of the Italian *cucina*.

SALSA DI POMODORO (TOMATO SAUCE)

1 kg good-quality canned, peeled tomatoes
or 1 kg ripe tomatoes, peeled

120 ml olive oil

2 cloves garlic, finely chopped

1 large onion, finely chopped

120 g tomato paste

sea salt and freshly ground black pepper

250 ml water

4 basil leaves

½ cup freshly chopped oregano

1 bay leaf

30 g butter (optional)

Bring a large pot of water to the boil. If using fresh tomatoes, score the bases with a sharp knife and put in the pot. Allow the water to return to the boil, then drain immediately. Wipe out the pot, add the olive oil and garlic and cook over a moderate heat for a few minutes. Add the onion and fry until it begins to colour. Stir in the tomato paste and cook for 2–3 minutes, stirring occasionally so it doesn't stick and burn. Add the tomatoes, season, and mix well. Pour in the water, bring to a boil and reduce the heat. Add the herbs and simmer gently for approximately 1 hour or until the sauce reduces to your required consistency and the tomatoes have all broken up. Pass the sauce through a food mill or strain through a fine sieve. Stir in the butter, if desired. ❧ *Makes 1 litre*

BESCIAMELLA (BÉCHAMEL SAUCE)

1 litre milk

½ small onion

1 bay leaf

1 clove

80 g butter

80 g flour

sea salt and white pepper

a grating of nutmeg

Put the milk, onion, bay leaf and clove in a saucepan. Warm over a moderate heat until simmering. Remove from the heat and rest for 15 minutes to allow the flavours to infuse. Melt the butter in a heavy saucepan, then add the flour and stir with a wooden spoon until the mixture forms a smooth paste (a roux). Cook, stirring continuously, for 2–3 minutes, taking care not to colour the roux. Strain the milk (discard the other ingredients) and stir it into the roux. Bring to a boil, beating vigorously to avoid lumps. Season with salt, pepper and nutmeg and simmer very gently for 10 minutes. ❧ *Makes 1 litre*

MAIONESE (MAYONNAISE)

3 egg yolks

1 teaspoon Dijon mustard

40 ml white-wine vinegar

900 ml olive oil

sea salt and freshly ground black pepper

Whisk the egg yolks, mustard and vinegar in a large bowl. Whisking constantly, slowly drizzle in the oil, at first drop by drop. The mixture will thicken and have a dull appearance. If it looks glossy, check to see that the oil is mixing in properly. To check if the mayonnaise has emulsified, dip a spoon in and look at the back of the spoon. If oil is floating on the top and the yolks have separated, add a little warm water to bring the mixture back together. Season with salt and pepper to taste. You should have a thick mixture in which a spoon will stand upright. If not, whisk in some more oil and adjust the flavour by adding a little more vinegar. ❧ *Makes 1 litre*

SALSA AGRESTO

120 g blanched almonds

1/2 clove garlic

1 cup freshly chopped flat-leaf parsley

1 teaspoon sea salt

a grind of black pepper

90 ml extra-virgin olive oil

90 ml verjuice

Preheat the oven to 220°C. Spread the almonds evenly on a baking tray and roast for about 5 minutes, shaking the tray occasionally to ensure even roasting. Allow to cool. In a mortar and pestle, crush the garlic, parsley, salt and pepper to a fine paste, using a little olive oil to smooth and lubricate the mixture. Add the almonds a few at a time with the remaining olive oil and the verjuice, until the mixture is well incorporated. ∾ *Makes 300 g* NOTE: The flavour of the sauce will vary depending on the type and quality of your olive oil. For example, you may prefer to use an oil with a nutty or grassy flavour.

BRODO DI POLLO (CHICKEN STOCK)

1 kg chicken bones, washed

4 litres cold water

1 onion, roughly chopped

1 carrot, roughly chopped

1 stalk celery, roughly chopped

1/2 leek, roughly chopped and well washed

1 bay leaf

1 sprig thyme

handful of parsley stalks

4 black peppercorns

1 teaspoon sea salt

Drain the chicken bones and put them in a large pot with the remaining ingredients. Heat gently until simmering, skimming the surface of any impurities. Simmer for approximately 3 hours, taking care not to let it boil rapidly, as this will make the stock go cloudy. Remove the pot from the heat and taste; the stock should have a distinct flavour of chicken. Gently strain into a container and use as needed. ∾ *Makes 3 litres*

BRODO DI PESCE (FISH STOCK)

1 kg fish bones

2 teaspoons butter

1 small onion, roughly chopped

1 bay leaf

1 tablespoon freshly chopped dill

1 tablespoon freshly chopped coriander

handful of parsley stalks

4 black peppercorns

1 stalk celery, roughly chopped

1/2 leek, roughly chopped and well washed

200 ml white wine

4 litres cold water

1 tablespoon sea salt

Rinse the fish bones under cold running water to remove all blood and impurities. Chop roughly with a large knife, making sure to sever any spines. Melt the butter in a large pot and fry the onion until slightly soft. Add the fish bones, herbs and peppercorns and fry until the onion is fully soft. Add the celery and leek, then deglaze with the wine. Pour in the water, add the salt and simmer for 20–30 minutes. Remove from the heat and taste, adjusting the seasoning if desired. Strain into a container and use as needed. ∾ *Makes 3 litres*

BRODO DI CARNE (BEEF STOCK)

1 kg beef bones

1 onion, roughly chopped (including skin)

1 carrot, roughly chopped

1 stalk celery, roughly chopped

1/2 leek, roughly chopped and well washed

olive oil

1 bay leaf

1 sprig thyme

handful of parsley stalks

4 black peppercorns

2 tablespoons tomato paste

200 ml red wine

4 litres cold water

Preheat the oven to 200ºC. Put the beef bones in a baking tray and bake for 30 minutes until browned all over. Meanwhile, heat a little olive oil in a large pot and fry the vegetables until slightly golden. Add the herbs and peppercorns and stir in the tomato paste. Cook for 2–3 minutes, then deglaze the pan with the red wine. Discarding any fat and liquid in the baking tray, put the bones into the pot and add the cold water. Bring to the boil, then reduce the heat and simmer for approximately 6 hours or until the stock has reduced by 25 per cent, removing any scum that rises to the surface. Add more water if required. Remove from the heat and strain. Use the liquid as desired.

Makes 2 litres

DEMI-GLACE: To turn the stock into demi-glace, reduce by half over a low heat. You will have a glossy, concentrated sauce.

BRODO DI VITELLO (VEAL STOCK)

1 kg veal bones

1 onion, roughly chopped (including skin)

1/2 carrot, roughly chopped

1 stalk celery, roughly chopped

1/2 leek, roughly chopped and well washed

olive oil

1 bay leaf

1 sprig thyme

handful of parsley stalks

4 black peppercorns

200 ml red wine

4 litres cold water

sea salt

Preheat the oven to 200ºC. Put the veal bones in a baking tray with the vegetables and a little olive oil and bake for 20 minutes until browned all over. Leaving any fat or liquid in the baking tray, put the bones, vegetables, herbs and peppercorns into a large pot. Deglaze the tray with the wine and add to the pot. Pour in the water, add sea salt to taste and bring to the boil. Reduce the heat and simmer for approximately 4 hours, skimming off any oil or impurities that rise to the surface. Remove from the heat and taste, adjusting the seasoning if desired. Strain into a container and use as needed. *Makes 3 litres*

PASTA DOUGH

500 g flour

500 g durum-wheat semolina

6 eggs

salt

Mix the flours and tip onto your workbench. Make a well in the centre and add the eggs and a couple of pinches of salt. Add a little water, if necessary. Knead until the dough forms a large ball and is smooth to the touch. This will take 10–15 minutes (if you prefer, use an electric mixer fitted with a dough hook). Continue kneading for 10 minutes, then cover with a moist tea towel or plastic wrap and set aside to rest for 20 minutes. The dough should be pliable enough to work with, not too dry or too soft. Divide the dough into 2–3 pieces so it is easier to work with. Roll each piece out by pushing it through a pasta machine on the highest setting. Fold it in half and run through the machine again several times, folding each time. (If you do not have a pasta machine, use a rolling pin on a floured surface.) This process is called laminating. You need to laminate the pasta until it looks and feels silky smooth, like a baby's bottom. Adjust the setting on the pasta machine each time

and roll the pasta until it is 1–2 mm thick. Cut into your desired shapes for filling, or into long strips, such as for tagliarini, fettuccine, pappardelle etc. (If you do not have a pasta machine, roll up the sheet of dough and cut through it with a very sharp knife to make long pasta such as tagliarini.) Spread out the pasta on a floured tray and use on the same as day you make it.

↪ *Makes 1 kg*

CROSTINI (CROUTONS)

Crostini are not only a good way to use up day-old bread but a great accompaniment for pastes, purées and small antipasto items. Eat them at the beginning of a meal or just as a snack.

day-old baguettes, thinly sliced

extra-virgin olive oil

sea salt and freshly ground black pepper

Preheat the oven to 180°C. Arrange the bread in a single layer on an oven tray, drizzle with olive oil and season with salt and pepper. Bake for 5 minutes until the bread is dry and lightly coloured.

PATATE FRITTE (ITALIAN FRIED POTATOES)

This is the perfect marriage of flavours for cooking potatoes. I've tried others but something always brings me back to garlic and rosemary. I'm not sure whether that's my heart or my stomach talking! Traditionally served as a side dish, these but are lovely by themselves, too. Don't be scared to eat the garlic – it is amazingly sweet when cooked like this.

8 large waxy potatoes (preferably Spunta)

8 cloves garlic, unpeeled

3 sprigs rosemary

olive oil

sea salt

Bring a large pot of salted water to the boil. Peel the potatoes and boil until soft but still firm. Drain and cool in the pot (do not run cold water over them, then chop into large cubes. In a large, deep frying pan, heat a generous amount of olive oil to very hot (around 190°C, if you have a cooking thermometer). Add the potato, garlic and rosemary, in batches if necessary, and fry until a lovely golden colour. Drain on kitchen paper and season with salt. Serve immediately.

PASTA FROLLA (SHORTCRUST PASTRY)

1 kg flour

1 tablespoon salt

500 g softened butter

200 ml water

Put the flour and salt in a large bowl and rub in the butter until the mixture has a sandy texture. Add the water a little at a time and mix until you have a large, smooth ball. Knead for approximately 5 minutes, then wrap in plastic wrap and refrigerate for 30 minutes. Roll out to your required thickness and line your tart case, using the rolling pin to ease the pastry over the case. Push the dough into place with your fingers and trim the edges. To blind-bake, preheat the oven to 160°C. Line the pastry with foil and fill with dried beans or uncooked rice. Put the tart case on an oven tray and bake for 12–15 minutes if large, or 10–12 minutes for small tart cases. Allow to cool, then proceed according to recipe. ❧ *Makes 1.5 kg*

PASTA SFOGLIA (PUFF PASTRY)

500 g flour

1 teaspoon salt

300 ml cold water

400 g butter, cold but pliable

Sift the flour and salt together onto your workbench and make a well in the centre. Add the water gradually into the centre and hand-mix to make a paste. Knead until the dough is smooth and elastic, then form into a ball, cover with plastic wrap and leave to rest for 30 minutes. Sprinkle some flour on your workbench and roll out the dough evenly to form a 20 cm square. Put the butter in the centre of the square and fold over the dough to enclose it completely, making a square block shape. Refrigerate for 10 minutes. Roll out the pastry to form a 30 cm × 10 cm sheet approximately 1.5 cm thick. Fold the sheet into three and roll out again to the same size. Repeat the folding and rolling, then refrigerate for 10 minutes. Repeat this process until the pastry has been turned 6 times in total, each time folding it in a different direction to the last time. Refrigerate for at least 20 minutes before use. Cut off your required quantity of dough and roll out on a floured surface to a thickness of 1 cm. Cut to your desired shape with a sharp knife or cutter and put on a floured tray. To cook, bake at 180°C for 12–15 minutes, or proceed according to recipe. Any leftover dough can be wrapped in plastic film and frozen until required. Defrost it in the refrigerator overnight. ❧ *Makes 1 kg*

NOTES

- To obtain perfect puff pastry, the dough and the butter must be of the same consistency – cold but pliable.
- The butter must not be too rigid when it is put inside the dough.
- The pastry must be kept cold while resting, but not chilled for too long. Excessive cold will cause the butter to harden and crack the pastry.
- Each time the pastry is rolled out, it must be in a regular shape, i.e. keep the sides and ends parallel to each other and the thickness even.

SCIROPPO (SUGAR SYRUP)

1 kg caster sugar

1 litre water

Put the sugar and water in a pot and stir until the sugar has dissolved fully. Bring to the boil over a high heat and boil for 15 minutes. Remove from the heat and allow to cool. Store in a sealed container until ready to use. ❧ *Makes 1.5 litres*

CREMA PASTICCERA (PASTRY CREAM)

This delicious custard is the basis of many fillings for tarts and cakes. It is wonderful piped inside freshly cooked *bomboloni*.

8 egg yolks

250 g caster sugar

100 g flour

1 litre milk

1 vanilla bean

Whisk the egg yolks and sugar in a stainless steel bowl for 5 minutes until creamy. Add the flour and a little of the milk and blend until smooth. Heat the remaining milk in a saucepan to just before boiling point, then slowly whisk the hot milk into the egg mixture. Return to the saucepan and whisk until thick. Allow the mixture to cook gently for 2 minutes before removing from the stove. Cool. ∾ *Makes approximately 1.2 litres*

COTOGNE CONSERVATE
(PRESERVED QUINCES)

The longer you cook quinces, the darker red they become. You will be amazed at the change in colour. Cooked to this recipe, they can be used as a filling in a sweet tart or as an accompaniment for duck or pork. On a cheese platter they will complement both creamy and tangy flavours.

1 kg quinces

350 g caster sugar

2 star anise

1 cinnamon stick

4 cloves

approximately 1 litre water

250 ml white wine

You will need a sterilised screwtop jar with a capacity of 1 litre. Preheat the oven to 180°C. Peel each quince and put it in a large bowl of water with a touch of lemon juice. When all the fruit have been peeled, pat dry, cut in half and lay flat in a deep baking tray. Cover with the sugar and scatter over the spices. Pour in the water and wine so that the fruit is nearly covered. Cover with foil and bake for 3 hours until deep red. Remove from the oven and allow to cool a little. While still warm, transfer the fruit gently into the jar and cover with the liquid. Screw the lid on tightly and put the jar in a large pot. Cover with water and simmer for 30 minutes. Remove the jar and allow to cool at room temperature. Refrigerate after opening. The quinces will keep for at least 2 months.

CILIEGIE (GRAPPA-PRESERVED CHERRIES)

The first box of cherries for the season in Australia creates quite a stir. It is usually auctioned off for charity and fetches thousands of dollars. When cherries are a little cheaper, try preserving them in grappa and you will have them to eat until next season – if they last that long! Not only will the cherries take on the flavour of the grappa, but the grappa will become cherry-flavoured. You can add the flavoured grappa to sauces for meat, or mix a little into whipped cream to make sweet dishes that much more wicked. For a decadent dessert, serve the cherries with scoops of best-quality vanilla ice-cream.

700 g firm, ripe dark cherries (morello), stems removed

200 g caster sugar

300 ml grappa (40% alcohol or more)

You will need a sterilised screwtop jar with a capacity of 1 litre. Wash and drain the cherries well. Prick each cherry with a pin and pack into the jar with the sugar. Cover well with the grappa. Secure the lid tightly and put in a cool place for at least 2 months, up-ending the jar occasionally. Refrigerate after opening. The cherries will keep for months and will improve with age.

Acknowledgements

GUY GROSSI

To find satisfaction in what you do day by day is a blessing, and for this I am grateful. This book captures the spirit of Grossi Florentino through the beautiful story told by Jan and the alluring photography by Adrian of the wonderful food that has become our family trademark. It shows the essence of Italian life in Melbourne.

To all who have contributed – family, friends, suppliers, past owners, staff – and to my teachers, thank you. You are all so special, so important to Grossi Florentino. Special thanks to Julie Gibbs and her team at Penguin, and to all who have kept the front doors swinging for the past seventy-five years. *Grazie.*

JAN McGUINNESS

I don't want to die and go to heaven: I'd rather live forever – in Italy. Writing this book has been the next best thing, immersing me as it has in the hospitality, generosity and good humour of those who have worked and played at the Florentino down the years. The Grossi family, Guy and Elizabeth especially, have been outstandingly helpful and generous collaborators whose dedication to the task has ensured its hassle-free outcome. Grossi Florentino's friendly and professional staff have eased our way at every level, and I am particularly grateful to Jeanette Barker.

Thanks to Julie Gibbs of Penguin for responding so enthusiastically to the idea and to our editor, Katie Purvis, and designer, Leonie Stott, for their encouragement and support in executing it. A special tribute to Adrian Lander (and his assistant, Louise Dixon), whose photographic depiction of Grossi Florentino is so very simpatico.

Deserving of special thanks for sharing their memories and directing me to others who also proved helpful are Leon Massoni, the late George Tsindos, Raymond Tsindos, Andrew Tsindos, Lorraine Podgornik, Andrew Sinn, Tony Rao, Kenneth Park, Philip Jones, Peter Rowland, Trevor York, Elda D'Amico, Mario Mocellin, Marcello Bidesi, Jonathon Crawford, Charles Anzarat, Michael Zifcak, Mirka Mora, Georgina Weir, Silvano Bizzari, Lino Tommasoni, Virginia Hellier, Ronald Walker, Sam Maggiore, Sheila Scotter, Stefan Aralica, John Sherad, Bob Ashby, Tony Beddison, Claude Forell, Lillian Frank and Louise Lechte.

Others helped unknowingly by writing articles and books I have drawn on. I would particularly like to acknowledge Anne Latreille, Claude Forell, Celestina Sagazio, Tom Hazell and Rowena Stretton, and Mietta O'Donnell's *Mietta's Italian Family Recipes* and Allan Wynn's *The Fortunes of Samuel Wynn*.

Index

Entries in *italics* indicate photographs.